MW00619481

Remember,
You are never too old
to rewrite your future and
dream a new dream.
All my best,
Janet Cole
2015

The Unwritten You

Rewriting Your Future After Divorce or Loss of Spouse

JANET COLE

The Unwritten You

By Janet Cole

Cover & Interior Design: Silver Signet Graphic Design

www.silversignet.com

Project Management: Pottenger Press & Publicity

www.pottengerpress.com

Editor: First Glance LLC

ISBN: 978-0-9968148-0-5

Sunshine Publishing, LLC

First Edition

Printed in United States of America

"The secret of change is to
focus all your energy not on fighting the old,
but on building the new."

-Socrates

Table of Contents

Foreword

Unwritten You: Rewriting Your Future

The Dead of Night

I awake, my eyes slowly flutter open, and I cannot recall where I am. It's dark, a clock is ticking away each second in the background. As my eyes struggle to focus, I don't recognize the room. I am having trouble comprehending my surroundings. The walls are different, all the furniture has been rearranged, and there is no outside light rimming the curtains. For the most part, the room is nearly pitch black. The only thing I can hear besides the consistent ticking of the clock, is my breathing combined with my heart beating; slow, laborious, eerie beats.

Can I feel my body? Yes, I can feel the skin of my calf against the cool sheets of the bed. *But do my legs work?* I don't know. They aren't moving. *Is that because they can't? Is something keeping my body from moving?* A dense fog surrounds my mind, hugging my body, creating restlessness. Its enigmatic thickness in the air presses down on my limbs, penetrating my ears, and infiltrating my nose and lungs. My heart is heavy, so heavy. The great mass of darkness weighs down my chest and affects my breathing; my life source. *In-out-in-out*; I am breathing, but I've almost forgotten how. It is no longer an involuntary action, but one that I have to be conscious about. Intentional about. It is slow, deep, work.

My body melts away, little by little, as I lay in this strange bed. I once read that a person can go 4-6 weeks without eating food, but only 3-7 days without water. *When was the last time I ate something? Did I drink water yesterday? How much water or fluids have I consumed recently, a cup? A quart? No, not even a quart.* As I lay in this semi-state of paralysis, my mind starts to make sense of my surroundings, and the reason I am waking up in a foreign room. The question of "Where am I?" Leads me to reach out for my husband, my best friend. I feel nothing. I reach out farther across the expansion of the bed in the dark, expecting my hand to come into contact with solid flesh and bone, but again my effort is in vain. *Where is he?* I could face this strange world and overwhelming dark fog, if I knew he was there. Even if he were asleep, it would be enough to settle my nerves having him near. I would know that I am safe.

Wait a minute. What is it that my brain demands me to know, but I cannot remember? *Where is my husband, my partner, my best friend? He was right there a moment ago.* I can still smell the scent of his skin. I can sense the lingering impressions in the bed and pillow of his body filling the space next to me. He was just there, in those few, short moments between asleep and awake. I want to grasp that in-between conscious state again where I feel him close. My mind begins to scream as it begins to grasps answers to those very questions that are running rampant through my mind. It is as if the answers I am looking for are masked behind the windows of a train in the distance that it is hurtling its way towards me. Recognition fills my eyes as I squint to make out the details of the face of the train; chrome accenting the dark exterior. There it is. The answer is right there, rapidly accelerating towards me. *Why is my breathing changing?* Faster, faster, faster. My shallow breaths match the increasing rate of speed of the engine charging at me. As the locomotive collides with my consciousness, it shatters against the resistance to remember. Memories pang against the interior of my skull. He is gone. He is not returning. I am in a different bed, in a different room, in a different house, and he is not coming back. I am alone.

The pain of that awareness is too much. I cannot bare exploring further details, repetitive questions, answers that cannot be justified. There are no answers, at least the ones I want to hear and accept as truth. This unwanted reality constricts my breathing, holding my mind and body hostage, paralyzing my muscles that feed my will to go on. I cannot bare reality and consciousness right now. It screams in my face. It is too hard. I can't do this. It is easier to be engulfed by the darkness, swallowed up in unconscious sleep. I will deal with reality later. I am not strong enough yet. *Let go. Let go.* I relax and let my mind and body drift back to sleep, to a place that is easier to exist. *You must protect yourself, your mind, your heart.* Like Dorothy in *The Wizard of Oz*, when the wicked witch created the beautiful field of poppies to put her to sleep, so shall I drift back to a protective unconscious sleep, and attempt to face the reality of being alone, another day.

Divorce, death of a spouse, a breakup of a long term relationship is the ending of a chapter in your life, which seems unbearable at the time. In the song, "Fix You", by Cold Play it describes this dead of night and the feeling of being stuck in reverse. The day before, in the beginning, love and happiness waxed strong. Many enjoyable memories were formed and forever imprinted on your mind. How can one stop the ever-reeling movie of those memories that seem to keep playing over and over, stuck on repeat? Towards the end of the day, as the light began to dim, you knew there was a change. Perhaps one that you didn't want to recognize or accept. One that whispered the inevitable change was happening, like a terrible event in slow motion. One that seemed destined to transpire. One that undeniably reaffirmed the end was near.
And now, that light is gone, and the relationship is over. You are disorientated, directionless, and full of despair, anxiety and hopelessness. You have somehow been caught up in a tide heading toward a whirlpool and now you are circling the

drain. The pressure of the waves capture you, hold you captive and force you to the bottom in depths of sadness and gloom. How do you breathe? How do you survive this state? When you jump upwards to break free of the whirlpool, you are sucked back in and pulled back to the rocky bottom, like a vicious beast devouring it's pray. How do you find the will to keep fighting? Your strength is nearly gone and so is your oxygen. Just before extinction, you hear a still, small inner voice encourage you to reach out another direction, a direction you have never thought of before. You feel for a hold; a rock, grasping for a plant root, anything that you can grip and pull yourself out of the vicious cycle of the spin-out. You follow your instincts and grab a rock, and pull yourself side-ways along the bottom of the river and escape the deadly monster's clutches. As you lift your head and eyes instinctively upward, toward the surface and oxygen, light floods your surroundings and you realize you have survived the event and will live to see another day, another new sunrise. Gratefulness consumes your thoughts and feelings for the chance at a new life, a new chapter and a new beginning.

CHAPTER ONE

The Day Dawn Breaks

Hope: The first step towards getting somewhere is to decide that you are not going to stay where you are.

The beginning of dawn. The darkness from the dead of night, blankets the early morning making it seem void and empty; absent of light and color. As morning nears, your breathing seems slow, deep and deprived of oxygen. Your eyes are searching for any source of light. Just before you give up, the light begins to lift behind the mountains. You can see the thin rim of light break free from caged mountain tops, one ray after another. The lightened sabers awaken and reach from behind the dark shapes, stretching toward the sky. Hope returns, and your lungs begin to receive oxygen again. The light feeds your starving soul. Similar to the butterfly, dawn is proof that you can go through a great deal of darkness, yet become something beautiful.

Initially, I was in a fog of sadness. I zombied from one day to the next. I took care of tasks that I had to and put off the rest. My main goal was to wake, exist (even as an empty shell of a human), then wait for nightfall to let unconsciousness create an escape from my hidden prison of despondency.

Then one morning, I was up early teaching an indoor cycle class at the gym. It was still dark when the class ended and the participants left. I continued to ride the stationary bike for a while in the dark, and through the windows I could see a clear view of the mountains. At that point they were just midnight blue shapes against the dark, early morning sky. As I continued to pedal, I watched as the first sign of light illuminated the rugged peaks. Then, the tips of the mountains glowed as the sun shot past them and energetically chased the sky. That was the first moment that I appreciated the beginning of the day rather than dreaded it. Up to that point, the day meant I had to labor to keep my thoughts from drifting to past memories, hurt, issues of abandonment, fears of being alone and insecurities of my financial future. I typically had to dodge people, their whispers, questions, and uttered sympathies. In my fragile state, any split second could unlock a dam of emotions resulting in public loss of composure, showing the world how weak and pathetic I was for missing someone who clearly didn't appreciate nor respect me.

However, that morning, the sun's first rays were beautiful how they seemed optimistic to begin a new day with endless opportunities. I began to sense in the first rays of hope that I had the ability to begin a new chapter in my life, leaving the old behind. Socrates said, "The secret of change is to focus all your energy not on fighting the old, but on building the new." The sunlight penetrated my mind and body reaching the depths of my soul, like it reached for every inch of the sky. I felt enlightened about my own ability and power to restart right at that moment, and choose how the rest of my life's story would play out. No longer would I walk through another day in a trance nor let that past relationship steal any more of my precious life's time. I had things to accomplish and I would live true to what I knew deep inside my core, that I am a difference maker in this world whether a single, particular person chose to see it or not. That one bad chapter doesn't define the rest of my story. I get to choose how this story plays out, and the end is far from over. I realized that at any given moment I have the power to say, "This is not how the story is going to end." The journey of a thousand miles begins with the first step, and I was ready to take it. You can too.

In the movie, Shawshank Redemption, Morgan Freeman stated, "You got to get busy living or get busy dying."

From here forward, I choose to get busy living. Hind sight is 20-20. Someday everything will make perfect sense. However, for today, laugh at the confusion, smile through the tears, and keep reminding yourself that everything happens for a reason. Say to yourself, "This is my dawn after a long dark night. It is my day to do with it that I want, no longer enslaved by the chains of desolation, but liberated with renewed dreams of hope and a new life." This is the dawning of the *Unwritten You*.

Don't judge me by the chapter you just walked in on.

I felt like up to that point, I needed to tell people, "You aren't catching me at my best." However, I knew I was going to become me again; a better me after surviving the storm. I am a survivor, as you are a survivor. You can feel your mind and soul search for faith of a new day, a new beginning of hope for its promise of opportunity. Putting hope into action is courage. This courage builds day by day to renewed strength. Use that courage to feel stronger, be stronger and give off strength to others.

However, be aware that sometimes courage becomes a thick outer armor protecting you, hiding weaknesses and buffering pain. On the upside, it is what helps you get up in the morning and steam through tasks that need done. On the down side, it barricades your feelings and doesn't let people in. You may feel more guarded, as if you have instinctively placed a caution signal over your senses to surround and protect your heart. At times you may seem numb and unfeeling clothed in that armor, yet at other times you cannot keep the tears from flowing.

In the song, *Becoming*, by April McLean, she talks about becoming healed. She reflects on the bridges she left burning, and what she couldn't give... (during that dark time) she can give now because of what she has overcome. *Becoming* is a song that spoke to me as I was healing and becoming stronger. In the pages at the end of this chapter, write the song title and words that speak to you during this new dawn and new beginning of your life. Take a few minute to write the words so that when you see them, read them and hear them, you feel stronger and more assured that you will make it through the dark times, no matter what.

You cannot change the past. No matter how much you may want the painful memories of the experience to be stripped from your recollection, they are a part of you. However, over time you will begin to realize that you have control over your thoughts and your actions. When you begin to take ownership of those two things you begin moving in a forward direction. You may still feel the loss of the relationship. Another realization may be, that you begin to recognize that you may not have treated those close to you very well as you worked through the emotion during that dark time, and apologies may be in order.

Just reflecting and recognizing the state you were in, a shell of the person you once were, you realize the only thing you can change is yourself, your attitude, your thoughts, your words and your actions. The way you look at life and how you choose to live your life in an intentional, positive, and forward thinking way takes courage and conviction. Conviction is a fixed or firm belief of persuasion and faith that you are destined to accomplish great things and it is time to get busy. As a result you will become hope, you will heal and overcome the fear and shame the darkness represented. Even though you are beginning a new life, don't downgrade your dream to fit your current reality. Instead, upgrade your perspective, your conviction and your attitude to match your destiny. Align your path to the one you were destined to walk upon, by letting your courage outweigh your fear. The bravest people feel fear, they just don't let it stop them from becoming who they were born to be. You are a survivor. You know you are a survivor, you feel it deep in your bones.

Survivor

This is an excerpt of a song that my daughter, Alysia Henderson, wrote for this book. It captures some of the emotion each of us feel as we go through difficult times, with the cards life deals us sometimes. It points out that it is inside of us to go through those trials and come out stronger for it. I couldn't have stated it better for the theme of this book then, "...You have battled the storms and learned to swim." Here it is.

Life is like, the rolling tides
And no one can control the ocean
I know that there are days, where you can't see the light
And you can't feel anything but broken
There will be people, who walk into your life,
That break you down and tell you, you have no worth inside
I'm standing here, telling you they're wrong and they don't deserve the tears you've cried.
You are a survivor
You've battled through the storms and learned to swim.
The mountains they get higher,
But don't give up until you win....
We are the survivors!

You never need to apologize for how you choose to survive.

Surviving is getting up the next day, putting your feet on the floor and embracing the fact that you weathered the storm, faced the darkness and chose to begin a new chapter in your life. You have the ability to choose how long you wait and wander in the darkness. For some it doesn't take long and for others it does. The goal is to realize that life is fragile, and there will be dark times. However, you are a strong, talented, beautiful person with so much to offer, and new experiences are waiting to become new accomplishments and new memories. Sometimes, especially in your fragile stage, the choices you make are not always best. This will happen and you may feel like you "fall off the horse, over and over." The key is to look for that new sunrise, re-commit to your goals and try again. It is important to try and try again. When you make mistakes, it is important to own them rather than make excuses. Excuses weaken you, your integrity and most importantly your belief in yourself and limits and delays your progress. So, if and when you make a poor choice, own it, correct it, forgive yourself and move on making different and better choices for better outcomes.

New relationships seems to be one of the top questions on people's minds after a divorce or death of a spouse. "How long before dating again? Should you ever date or get serious again? How to open up and trust another person to have a healthy relationship." This book does not provide those answers, because every situation is different. My ex began dating the week I moved out, although technically he wasn't in a relationship. For me, I knew I wasn't ready for a relationship right away and spent the first year recuperating. I knew how much I was still grieving on the inside. I didn't want to date, although I didn't want to stay home alone with my sadness either and face the memories and my reality.

Two months after my separation, I realized that I still had two tickets to the City Chamber Annual Gala event. I had purchased them months prior with the plan to go with my (ex)husband. As it rapidly approached, I was faced with the decision to cancel and stay home or go solo. I wasn't ready to take a date publically to the event which would initiate having my networking business colleagues ask questions. In my private thoughts, I knew that the only person I wanted to go with was my soon to be ex-husband, but I wasn't going to let that get me down nor get the best of me on that day. So, I kept my hair dressing appointment, bought a new dress, beautified and went to the event. On the inside I was still grieving, but I knew I had to still live life. I chose to dress up, hold my head high and enjoy the experience. Unknowingly, I impressed a lot of people that night for my ability to be positive and strong. Since then, many of these same people have mentioned holding me as an inspiration for them as they go through their own dark times. You don't often get these opportunities back, so make the best of them. By accentuating the positive, and decreasing the negative, you can be a difference maker for people.

Another question I have received and experienced myself is, "How do you get up and adorn the strong armor to go on, but not keep others out?" What this means is, how do you put on a strong thick skin to get through the emotional times, yet not distance yourself from others? Being a survivor doesn't have to demand always being independent and self-sufficient. Friends forced me out of my comfort zone of wearing the mask of strength and happiness when in public. As a result, I found that it was ok to confidentially let your inner circle of friends see your authenticity. It is good to remove the armor and the mask once in a while and be genuine. You'll find that the bricks you use to create your heart's protective fortress can also trip you up. So, with people you trust, break down the barriers and embrace your hopes, concerns, anticipations and hesitations to gain clarity and perspective of where you are and where you want to go with close friends. Interestingly enough, it is when you let down your guard and exercise transparency, that your select few of friends in your inner circle have the ability to see past the armor to support, listen and care. On the other hand, when I wore a poker face and didn't let others penetrate my outer lining, people didn't let me in either. It can be very distancing and create pseudo or artificial friendships. However, when I was real, genuine and authentic, people connected with me, and related to me better.

Part of the hope of a new day is casting off the darkness, and sometimes that takes reaching bottom and choosing to begin climbing back up again. Going through the grieving process is necessary. Grief is the last act of love we have to give to those we loved. Where there is deep grief, there was much love. You may feel weak, scared, angry, hurt and damaged. Time will pass. Then as your light of consciousness dawns a new day, so does your determination to get up, get moving and begin changing your life.

One exercise to do daily is to take deep breaths. Try this: As you breathe in deeply, think "confidence" and as you breathe out, exhale feelings of insecurity. Try it again. Take in a deep breath and see yourself as strong and confident. When you exhale, get rid of doubt and discouragement that creates insecurities. Do that seven to ten times right now until you can feel a difference in your confidence level. Try standing up and lifting your arms above your head as you breath in and think positively. Journal at the end of this chapter the difference you feel when doing the breathing exercise. If you can, make it a part of your daily routine. As you do, visualize a new, confident you, and you will become that new, confident you.

Activity

In the Unwritten You program, there are meaningful exercises that will help you heal, shed the shadows to open up and trust others again to get close to you. One example, is an exercise designed to aid the dawn and make the darkness recede. Use the journal pages at the end of this chapter for the following exercise.

Activity: Out With the Old

Directions

1. Begin by writing the name of the person that hurt you.
2. Write down all the words that they made you feel poorly, unloved, unworthy etc.
3. Write down some of the most hurtful things that person said or acted toward you. For example: (Person's Name) would rather be alone and lonely than with me; that he would rather be poor than have my helpful income if it meant living with me. That somehow I caused his need for affairs.

The key is to write all those difficult things down on the paper. Then read them, see them for what they are-"just words". Those words carried so much hurt and emotion in the past. However, now you can cast away the darkness of those words and their attached emotion.

4. The final step is to rip up the piece of paper right out of the book. Go ahead. Tear each little scrap from this book. Rip and tear lightly or ferociously it is your choice. Rip it once, or take pleasure of ripping it into hundreds of little pieces. The meaning behind it is, they are just words on paper that cannot affect you or torment you any longer- throw them away and cast off the darkness.

Dispose of the paper. Burn, flush, shred or drop them in the nearest waste basket.

You have purged yourself of that negativity and will need to replace that empty space with something positive. It isn't enough to discard the negative words, you have to replace them with positive words. We will do a number of activities in this book to replace the old with the new and adopt positive words and thoughts to replace the negative ones. Take pride and confidence in yourself and your value and self-worth. You will hear me repeat these words again in other chapters. You need to hear them repetitively.

When studying to become a teacher many years ago, I read that it takes approximately 25 repetitions to transition knowledge from short term to long term memory. It takes approximately eight times of doing something correctly to remember the process. Hear, read, speak and think these words until you adopt them: You are strong, courageous and still a difference maker. Perhaps your positive influence ended temporarily with the person from your past, but you have the ability, in time, to find someone you can make an even better difference with together. You have a bigger purpose to fulfill. It is time to believe it, look for it, find it and fulfill it.

My grandmother, Rachel Martindale, who lived to be just a few hours short of 96 years old, was a widow for 37 years. I know that she is from a much earlier generation, which supported having one husband and not remarrying. However, today it is different and is much more accepted in society to remarry. Right now it may seem impossible to even fathom finding someone new to trust, care for and live out your days with. At this stage you may still be jaded and cautious about ever getting into a relationship again. Nevertheless, the beauty of it is you have time; You have a new day and new life to go at your own pace. My grandmother chose to focus on loving up her approximate 40 grandchildren, 80 great grandchildren and 16 great-great grandchildren with 4 more on the way. Her shining light was her family, her legacy and her reason for living. Her passion for her family was strong and lasted 37 more years on this earth.

The key to your light is your "why". You have to find your "why" for moving on and rewriting your future. Perhaps it is because being a parent, grandparent and great grandparent is your why. Perhaps it is the difference you make at work and your career. I encourage you to get a journal to write in every day, outside of the few pages that are included at the end of the chapters in The Unwritten You. Each morning as you write in your journal the things you are grateful for, begin identifying your "why" for the day. Perhaps thinking and journaling your "why" creates positive anticipation for your day, as well as helps you get prepared to meet and execute the tasks and events creating a more successful day.

Volunteering and serving others may give you your why. I was always told, and I believe it, that no matter how hard our life or trials seem to be, if we take a look around us and observe what other people are enduring, it doesn't take long before we realize our problems are small. We are pretty lucky compared to a lot of people and what they are going through. There is a saying that "hurt people, hurt people". I believe that is true for those that are stuck. You can help yourself and others by putting the opposite emotion into action. I truly believe that when you are hurting, if you can find a way to provide a service to help someone it will turn your sadness around and get you out of your funk. Perhaps someone in your neighborhood is moving, or someone sick needs a meal or a single mother with young children needs a break or her house cleaned. The moment you look outward and become perceptive of other people's needs and serve another person, your light grows and shines and casts out the shadows of lingering pain. Even more importantly, your ability to love increases which helps heal you from the inside out.

Reflection is a good exercise during healing and leads us to look inward at ourselves and learn from our experiences, our issues of conflict and resolution. Then in time, it is important to take our focus off ourselves, from looking inward, and turn it outward toward the light by helping other people. Service is one answer to the question, "After a devastating event as an unwanted divorce, break-up or death of a spouse how do we find hope for a new dawn to carry us through?" The first step is working through the process of grieving. Everyone must go through it in order to move forward. One cannot take this lightly nor skip over steps in the process. As with dealing with a loved one passing, a break up or divorce is similar because it is a death of a relationship. There are many things we cannot control. With service toward another person, be mindful that love and compassion in your heart toward someone is an opportunity to make a difference in that person's life. You must learn to follow that love. Don't ignore it, act on it. Somebody needs the caring, skills, and help that you have to give. Always leave people better than you found them. Hug the hurt, kiss the broken, befriend the lost, and love the lonely. If you do, you will be filled with more light, casting out the shadows, which will help you get through the grieving process.

I have a hometending business of placing a responsible occupant in a vacant property to secure and maintain it. With this business, in addition to my real estate business, my tag line for years used to say, "Making a difference, one property at a time." Now, after this life lesson that I learned, I realize it is more about people helping people. The physical property is an object, the person is the lesson and emotion that will echo and last forever. This resonated in what I experienced and learned during my 20+ years teaching junior high, in the public school system. "What you teach me I will remember for a day, how you made me feel I will remember for a lifetime."

Mindset

A new day begins with a new mindset. The moment you wake up, you begin the pattern of your day by your first thoughts. This a great time to write in your journal. It sets the stage and precedence for your whole day. As you write, if you cannot think of a positive thing to think about, begin with being grateful for the privilege to simply be alive and healthy. The moment that you begin your day with the realization that life is a gift and a blessing, you will begin to believe it. Time spent appreciating, is time worth living. It begins with your thoughts. If the tragic event is the dark, mountainous shapes, our positive, reflecting thoughts are the sunrays that begin to rim the caps and stretch beyond their damning efforts to hold you back. Waking up, being grateful that you did wake up is a start. You are still alive and have the ability to have this day to do with it as you will. Life is a gift. Yesterday is the past and cannot be changed, tomorrow is the future and has no guarantees. However, today is tangible and can be molded and sculptured by your own hands. You can choose to lay in bed an extra hour and enjoy the quiet, reflective time. Or you can choose to sit up, grab a pen and begin writing down the things you want to accomplish in your day. How you plan, makes such a difference with what you accomplish in the 24 hour time that you have been given.

In Greek Mythology, there is story of Pandora's Box. Briefly, the story is that a midst of darkness and evil escapes Pandora's Box, flooding the earth with the plague of sickness, pain, hurt, jealousy, and hate. The certain death and extinction of man seems absolute, futile. Then, light begins to eat away the darkness; slowly, deliberately penetrating the black pockets. As the initial rays awaken, stretch and rise up into the sky, so does hope, love and the need for survival. The light of hope is the abstract sword that slashes the fog and darkness. Even today, as in Pandora's time, if man opens his mind and heart to hope, multiplying belief, love, forgiveness and gratefulness, then the darkness has no choice but to resend to the corners of the earth. Corral the shadows lurking in our minds and hearts and kill them with light.

Renew hope daily. It isn't easy to go to war on the defeating darkness. Deciding to wake up, sit up, and to swing your legs over the side of the bed and set them on the floor does not give your muscles the strength to stand let alone walk. Sometimes, there are people in your life that give you the support to stand up and test your strength and balance. Usually after a devastation like the one you have experienced, you are too week to stand alone. Good friends, children or grandchildren, your job, hobbies, etc. are your crutches to hold you up as you begin to grow stronger again. Hope of a new day, a new dawn, a new beginning is the optimism you use to lift your head and face life. It gives you the aspiration and eagerness to ask, "Why not me?" I agree with you; It is your turn to flourish, to yearn for something better, happier and more productive. You deserve to find happiness. Make that your ambition. Now is the time to take back the power over your own life, giving you the freedom to begin the blank page to begin rewriting your future, *The Unwritten You*.

Freedom

Freedom is mine, the sun in the sky, the breeze drifting by knows how you feel. You are stronger, and looking forward to the opportunity to do something different with your day and build upon a new life. A song that initiated my first "aha moment" and began to let in the sunlight is "Feeling Good" sung by Michael Buble. Whether it is a bird, the sun, a butterfly, your close friend or a perfect strangers in the grocery store, it will be apparent to them that you are feeling good. What song speaks freedom to you? Listen to it again now and include some of the words and main phrases in your journal pages at the end of this chapter.

Freedom comes from letting go of hurt and negative emotion. It also comes from breaking free in a forward movement. In this book, you will be given ideas to help you achieve freedom from that which is holding you hostage, stuck in reverse. You may not know you are stuck, or even have been for a long time. Here is an example.

One morning shortly after the separation, once again I was rushing in to teach the early morning cycle class at the gym. Imagine me running in with no make-up, lack of sleep lending itself to puffy, dark circles under my eyes, and hair thrown in a ponytail. I don't know if my socks even matched. I was going through the motions with a heavy heart, a broken heart that I didn't want to let anyone see or be privy to. That morning when I walked into the room, Debbie, one of the regular participants said, "Something about you has changed." I told her I didn't know what she meant, and she explained that my countenance had changed. She said that she noticed that months earlier, I had given off a stifled and oppressed countenance. *Even before the end of the relationship?* I thought.

She said that earlier that year (perhaps during the sunset of the relationship) I had a countenance that seemed oppressed and weighed down and gray. Now, however, in that moment it was lighter, brighter even in a dark spin room. I was amazed that she was perceptive to see something that even I had not observed, that months ago the relationship was afflicted and in distress; suffering so much, that people could see it so easily. I was relieved that day, even in the midst of my bewilderment, that even in what I thought was the darkest time in my life, the rays of dawn were beginning to appear again. That my mind and personal glow was lightening, so much that others could tell it even in the dimly lit corner room of the gym.

Balance

Balance means being intentional about giving time and effort to renew and regenerate yourself, relationships with others, commitments at work, and stimulate the mind and feed the spirit. There is hope for a new future. One that we individually have the opportunity to take the reins and make decisions about. Take it in baby steps strides. With each step, let your mind feed on the possibilities of what you can do with your new life. During this process, make sure to take time to feed the mind, the soul and your commitment to continue your recovery. This may include an hour in the bubble bath, or perhaps an early morning walk, run or hike to greet your day. There are many ideas to rejuvenate your spirit and initiate excitement of the day ahead of you. It is imperative to balance the demands that are placed on you. This is still a fragile time in your life. Each and every day, take time to give back to yourself and recharge your batteries in some way. Journaling daily blessings, aspirations and items of gratefulness is a wonderful start. Taking in your beautiful surroundings and setting time aside to ponder and reflect is another.

Activity

In the pages at the end of this chapter, journal about balance. List the things that help you to recharge your batteries and achieve balance.

Later in this book, we will discuss many tools to help you look and feel your best from the inside out, and to continue recharging your batteries. Imagine your emotional strength as a solar battery that gets recharged regularly in the sun to continue to power your physical and mental actions to a better life. So, staying busy with kids/ grandkids, friends, family, work and colleagues will help strengthen you, but you have to make sure to take time to rejuvenate yourself in order to recharge those solar batteries. Reading a good entertaining book (I call mind candy), or personal development book or podcast can give you new ways of looking at yourself, your relationships, and being the best individual you can be.

Sometimes this can be as simple as an inspirational thought or message from a website or Facebook friends. If you find a good one that speaks to you, share it; save it; post it and re-read it. Believing that you have a better life waiting for you, a life that you can choose how to construct ignites the hope to move forward. With each hour, get a dose of sunlight both physically and mentally. Stand in the sunshine with your face toward the heavens. Go pick out and purchase 3 full outfits that begin the change of the new you. Donate some of the old clothes, pictures, etc. that remind you of your old life-the life before the darkness. Begin your day in a new outfit. On a whim, stop by the mall and select new make-up or cologne. You deserve it. It is part of your new, fresh look. As people notice that you are renewed and refresh, you can let them know of the new dawn, the new day, and spread the good news of your new, empowering life you are both living and embracing.

Activity

In the journal pages at the end of this chapter, write or glue in the phrases, poems, pictures etc. that speak to you. If you truly believe that you have a better life waiting for you, what does that look like? Write it down, cut out pictures of what it looks like and put them in your journal to reflect upon every time you flip through the pages.

This is also a wonderful time to renew old friendships with friends and family. Write letters, send emails, text something positive to at least one person a day and just watch as the light of dawn affects, improves and renews other relationships. The key is to be the kind of person you want to attract in a friend or partner. So as this new day begins and you are rewriting your future, let's do the next exercise.

Directions: Make a list of characteristics that would be

important to you in a confidant, a best friend, or a partner. Narrow those characteristics down to your top 10.

	Characteristics	Why is it important to you?	How do you rate?
1.			
2.			
3.			
4.			
5.			
6.			
7.			
8.			
9.			
10.			

Rate your own characteristics as a friend or partner. Where are your strengths and your weaknesses? Identify the areas you need to improve on to not only be the kind of person you want to spend time with, but also be the type of person with qualities you seek and want to attract. Spend some time in your journal expanding on these qualities, what they look like and why they are important to you.

The next exercise is to think of Winnie the Pooh. He was a nonjudgmental friend to everyone in the forest. In your journal pages, list the qualities you like in the character Tigger. For example, he was bouncy, energetic, happy, and laughed a lot. Now think about the donkey Eeyore's qualities. He feels sorry for himself, he whines, his voice inflection always pitches down, and he is depressing. If you had the choice, which character would you rather spend time with? Which character of those two would you rather others identified in you? There is no right or wrong answer. The answer simply is to choose this new dawn to become the person you want to be and you want to attract. Don't just give lip service to it. Act it, own it and believe it.

Attitude of Gratitude

Thoughts precede action. Day dawn, hope for that new life, is where it begins. You have to renew that hope over and over throughout your morning, mid-day and afternoon. As previously mentioned, it begins with your first thoughts in the morning. For example, recognize that it feels good to breathe, the sheets against your body are smooth and cool, or that bubble bath feels luxurious. You appreciate the sounds of the birds, the light streaming through your window, the movement and bustle in the neighborhood, the way the sun streams across the sky on your morning walk, the fact that you have friends and family that love you, or the way the flowers open toward the sun and give off many bright colors that bring you pleasure to see and smell. It is important to begin each day, being thankful for life, good health and the ability to create your own happiness. When married, did you ever notice that when your spouse was happy, you were happier too? If my spouse was stressed or upset, I could feel it affect my mood. When you spend a great length of time serving the one you love, and walk by their side, you sometimes tend to mirror their emotions. The simple fact that you can wake, open your eyes and become cognoscente of your own thoughts and feelings separate from anyone else's is part of the beginning of a new dawn for you. You are breathing, feeling, thinking and acting separate from anyone else and that is an investment in you and your future. Take a moment right now and reflect how you are feeling and why.

In conclusion of this chapter, nothing is as dramatic as the dawn, when the new light begins to appear and grow. That is the turning point in your life that you will remember. You had faith the sun would come up, that life would go on and it did. It is important to keep a journal of your thoughts, feelings and experiences at this time. Not only will you find "aha" moments from putting your thoughts on paper, but being able to have a record to go back and reflect on at a later time will be advantageous and a growth experience you can measure over time. Record in your journal the moments when you first started to feel the light, feel a change. Right down the song you heard or the saying you read that may have acted as a catalyst and revisit it. Remember the movie, *City of Angels*, where the angels congregated to face the East and watch the sunrise. There was music that accompanied the rising of the sun and new day. As the beginning rays of dawn grow, so does your renewal of hope. It is a new dawn, it is a new day, and it is the beginning of a new life for you. It is the first chapter of The *Unwritten You*.

The Day Dawn Breaks

Date ____________

Date ______________

Chapter Two

The Sun Rises

Honor: "This old world is a new world and a bold world for me. Freedom is mine..."

You have taken another step in the closure of a past chapter in your life. Looking back, you recognize the happiness in the memories of that day, and it is ok to treasure those memories. You also recognize that as the day began to wain, and those times became part of the past and the darkness settled in, that chapter closed, only to open a new chapter and a new day in your life. It didn't burst into direct sunlight right away. That happened over time, just like healing of the past happens slowly but surely over time. More light creeps in and your eyes open to a new day, a new dawn and it is all for you. It is attainable. It is something you deserve and can wrap your mind around. There are and will be times you are sad and may even feel guilty that you are moving on. Perhaps, it feels as though you are cheating the memories of yesterday or the person in the past by living, breathing and boldly taking steps to proceed in a forward motion gaining momentum. Nonetheless, you can get past that thinking and realize that moving on is in your best interest. It is how you will survive.

Recenter-Refocus

There are also times, when you look around and the wonderment of how you came to be in this situation overwhelms your senses and leaves you disoriented. In that moment, stop, re-center and refocus. How do you re-center and refocus? Simple, it is a step that you have already learned:

Think of the wonderful blessings of life, people and new memories you are creating. Now open your eyes and search for the light that hovers and lights your path by reviewing and refocusing on the goals you want to achieve. Move, once again, in that direction.

How do you re-center when the shadows appear? One idea is to call a friend that is a good listener. Let them hear you out, including the guilt or momentary sadness you are feeling, and give them opportunity to validate those feelings for you. Another is to re-write your goals and what it is you are working to accomplish, including the stepping stones toward achievement. Sometimes looking at the closest stepping stone and committing to leap to, is enough to get you out of your funk and moving again.

Another idea to re-center is to write powerful words of affirmation in your journal, on paper or notecards that you can pin up and keep in sight. In your strong moments, write things that you like about yourself, including who are you at your core? Sometimes our outer strength, our armor is a reflection of who we really are. For example, people saw my armor as tough, durable, and mostly impenetrable. That armor, at times, kept me from falling down and falling apart. Each day, I would rise and put on my armor to face the day.

Was that independent, self-sufficient outer shell really me or who I wanted the world to see? After much reflection, and reaching rock bottom, I discovered on my journey out of the darkness that the armor of strength, independent, and self-sufficiency was my outer casing for courage. So, courage is at my core. Also, the years I spent trying to get validation from others was unnecessary because I was born honorable. Honor is at my core. In addition, through the good times and bad, the darkness and the light, gratefulness has always been at my core and what has pulled me through. It has been my saber to slice through the depths of sadness and despair. To find things I am grateful for, has always helped me find my "Why" for continuing forward. My courage, honor and gratitude are the reasons why I can find my new dawn. Sluff off the old world and begin a new one. Do not forget the old world, people, experiences etc., instead learn from them.

Recently, I was visiting with my father about it being a year since my divorce. I told him that if I had the opportunity to go back to the moment where I walked up and introduced myself to my ex-husband for the first time, I used to think I would take it, and miss that meeting that set events in motion. Now, after a year of reflection I accept the words that, "Everything happens for a reason." I realize that if I had not experienced both the love and the tragedy of that relationship, I would not be the person I am today. I would not have the perspective nor would have had opportunities to learn and grow. I would not have written this book, and have the opportunity to help other people with the knowledge and experiences I have had. So, from that perspective, I am grateful for my life lessons, the good, the bad and the ugly. I embrace them, I own them as mine and I will continue to learn from them.

Activity

At this point, stop and do the breathing exercise again. It is important to replace negative thoughts with more positive ones as we know. In addition, the breathing action is a TPR (total physical response) which combines putting the thought with an action initiating purpose and closure. Here we go: Breath in appreciation for this life lesson. Breathe out hurt. Breathe in strength, breath out weakness. Breathe in ownership, breathe out being a victim. Breathe in decision making, breathe out excuse making. Do this over and over seven to ten times as needed until you feel like you are the captain of your own ship, your ship of life, rather than a dingy being tossed to and fro, helplessly, with the current.

Each of us is a recipe full of ingredients gleaned from life's experiences. Like in reality, sometimes we can trade out an ingredient such as using applesauce instead of butter, if we feel it is a better, healthier choice. Simalarly, we are made up of our ingredients and our seasoning. Keep in mind, the reason why we love ourselves and others love us is because of who we are and all the experiences we have lived, felt and made a part of us along the way. Our new world is partly made up of the knowledge of the old world and everything we saw, felt, thought, said and did. Use this knowledge, make different decisions. Always be looking for new, better and healthier ways of doing things. Having options is powerful, especially when we have wisdom and experience to back it up.

You gain more freedom as you honor yourself. How do you honor yourself, your future, and your new day? When you are honoring yourself, people will notice a different light in you. They may not be able to put their finger on it, and may say your presence is happier or brighter. All of it is true. As you progress day by day, you are practicing and taking steps to be a happier, more grateful person that honors yourself. As you have learned, appreciating time, opportunity and letting go of hurt, sadness, anger and resentment and replacing it with joy and happiness, honors you. As you honor yourself, others will want to spend time with you. You will find they admire your strength and have a desire to be more like you because you exemplify intentionally living. You have ownership of your own star to guide your steps, and as a result you experience more freedom.

When you honor yourself, you are able to better

control your emotions, bridle your passions and slay your shadows. Since reading this book, strive to become more of a goal setter, developing a more focused and determined you. If you learn to seize your day, capture opportunities and decrease negative thoughts, it can eliminate procrastination from your vocabulary that can set back your goals and dreams for an indefinite amount of time. As you take control back, if you set your goals with realistic time frames to match and make the most out of your day you will gain the freedom of choosing what you accomplish. As a result, even the sun, the breeze and the butterflies floating on by know how you feel...which is pretty good.

Fear

Fear feeds insecurity, which is an opposite emotion of confidence. Confidence is what you have been working towards to become stronger and more determined during the last several weeks, months and years since the "dead of night". However, fear is not the paralyzer that people make it out to be. It can set you back, feed the shadows to grow and encompass your emotions and throw you off track. However, fear is also a good temperature gauge. Fear is not to be feared, it helps you know that you are doing something out of the norm, stepping out of complacency. It takes stepping out of your comfort zone to embrace change. Fear is felt when the realistic voice inside your mind reminds you that you have to get all your ducks in a row and you have to be prepared before charging forward into your future. Fear communicates that you are taking steps and leaps forward, and at times it may be uncomfortable.

You have triggers and baggage of emotions attached to experiences in your past that make you fearful of taking steps in your present and your future that may end in the same result; getting hurt. How do you make a change to do something different, get something different and avoid getting hurt? Take the knowledge of your past, re-evaluate your choices and your actions that ended in a way other than you wanted, and change it. Change the equation. If you want a different result you have to change up the variables that got you there. However, you have to trust again to grow and move forward, and sometimes that means getting hurt. There are no guarantees, but if you don't love and trust again, you will always be stuck.

For nearly 15 years, I coached junior high volleyball players. I taught them that the end result is directly affected by how you begin. So when you begin, you have to have the desired end or outcome in mind. The athletes practiced all the scenarios and combinations of each action to process through to get the desired result. If the different players were unprepared, they may not know what job they need to do, or task to perform to get the ball strategically over the net. If they let fear, doubt or insecurities paralyze them, they wouldn't be able to move their feet to the ball to put them into position to take the best action of attack against their enemy. In this case, the phrase, "Feel the fear and do it anyway", comes into play. Just like an athlete instinctively moving toward the ball to execute the play efficiently, we need to automatically do what needs to be done, to strategically reach the desired end result. Each action has a consequence and for every action there is a reaction. Productivity will result if you start your day determined to be strong, grateful, and determined to get the most out of it. Identify the fear, analyze it and break through it. You will find yourself victorious on the other side. Here is the equation: Determination + Attitude + Gratefulness = Productivity.

HONESTY

One way you find yourself victorious on the other

side is to be true to yourself. Take time to be transparent and authentic not only with others but with yourself. That takes honest reflection. If you looked back at business situations that went south or relationships that ended badly, you will find ways you could have done things differently, made different choices, treated people differently or more genuinely. The golden rule of treating others like you want to be treated rings true here. My paternal grandmother, Kathryn Cole, counseled me when I was a younger girl about being honest. She would have me imagine how the world would be so different if everyone was just honest; Honest in their dealings with their fellow man and honest with themselves. One way to be honest with yourself is to realize that you are not infallible, nor does the strong unpenetrating armor you walk around in throughout your day keep you untouched or represent who you are. You can still be hurt. Your underlying feelings are still raw and fresh. Surround yourself with people in your inner circle that you can be honest with. Be yourself, be vulnerable.

Also be honest with yourself on the progress you are making and want to make. Reflect if you are feeling strong and ambitious that day, or feel the need for a slower paced, more quiet and reflective day. Be honest about the shadows that are cast, and the struggles with them and the joyous celebration when you have once again beaten them and cast them off. Being honest is an honorable trait. It is what leaders and true leadership is founded on. Being dishonest belittles you in your eyes and in the eyes of those around you. So, take ownership of your decisions, both in the past and present so that you can make sound decisions and changes for your future. Being honest takes courage, which is faith in action for a better new day and gives you freedom.

Courage, honor and gratitude are the reason why you can find the new dawn, the new day and it is yours for the taking. Remember, even the bravest of creatures have some fear, but it is not enough to stop them from moving in the path they are destined to walk upon. What is your path? Remind yourself who you were destined or born to be. Understanding this and figuring out who you are will help you understand where you are going and what you can accomplish.

The Core

In one of my other upcoming books called, *The Core*, I take you into more detail of cutting through the layers to discover your core. It is a rewarding process. Here is a small example of the meaningful and affective exercises we do in The Core.

Activity

Now turn to journal page at the end of the chapter showing in your book and begin writing words that you know about yourself.

1. What words describe you at your core? Who were you born to be? As a child, you were untarnished, unblemished and innocent. You had your whole life to learn, grow and decide who you wanted to be. However, in that fresh, new mind and body, who and what were you? These are the gift of personality traits you were born with, to take into the world to make a difference for you and others.

Select 3-5 words from the following list, or come up with your own.

Strong	Vibrant	Valiant
Honest	Honorable	Caring
Kind	Passionate	Authentic
Genuine	Courageous	Nurturing
Respectful	Humble	Thankful
Grateful	Supportive	

2. Transfer your words to the journal pages. Write at least one paragraph about each of the words your have chosen and the reason for choosing that word to describe your core.

3. Transfer the words you have chosen to truly describe you under your armor and without the mask, to note cards that you can strategically place throughout your home, in your car, at work, or in your wallet/purse. It is important to read and remember day by day as you

take steps to rewrite the future you want to have and is deserving of someone with these traits.

4. At this time, write a page in your journal how your core has influenced your life so far. Can you see it in the profession you have chosen or how you interact with your children, family, neighbors or friends? Explain in your journal how you think these qualities and characteristics can influence your new future, how you are at work, or new activities you choose to participate in or people you choose to interact with. These qualities are not a mask, they are inside every fiber of your being. Use this knowledge to walk the path you are destined to walk upon and prepares you for who you are to become. The time is now to become a difference maker in the world. Rewrite your future to your fullest greatness and potential.

In conclusion of this chapter, honor yourself by realizing that you are made up of all the experiences you have gone through on your journey so far. Be grateful for those experiences because they have shaped and molded you into the person you are now. Yet you are more mindful and smarter about doing things differently for a different outcome from here forward. You are ready to take on the mantle, and accomplish a great work you were born to do. You are a difference maker at the very core of your being and it is time to make the world a better place by the people you encounter and positive influence you can have on others. You have to find your "Why" your passion to do what you set out to do. Your heart beats with the potential to do great things and you feel it in your inner intuition that you are capable of doing it. You can hear your inner voice whisper that you were born to do great things, and you are re-writing your future to include those and become your destiny.

The Sun Rises

Date ______________

Date ____________

Date ____________

Chapter Three

Shadows

Gratefulness: "Keep your face to the sunshine and you will not see the shadows." Helen Keller

As the light begins to grow stronger, you remember glimpses of yesterday; memories of days past. Perhaps you aren't expecting it, but you find yourself standing in a place where the ghost of a memory echoes through your consciousness. A favorite song plays on the radio at a restaurant or store, recollection of a word or phrase you used to say, or someone walks by that looks like the person you have lost. Your breath catches in your throat, your heart pounds as the paralyzing shadow of a distant memory holds you motionless until it passes over you. Without realizing it, you have been holding your breath and your eyes are fixed as the memory saunters across your mind. Finally, after being held hostage in the moment, you are released. Surroundings begin to form and take shape again as you look up into the sky; the shadow has past.

Even though you have made the decision to move forward, looking through the windshield of life rather than the rearview mirror and grow stronger, there will be times when the shadows catch you off guard and take you by surprise. Similar to a large airplane crossing the sky, or the sun hiding behind the dark gray clouds, the shadows will appear and linger.

At times it seems easier and safer to return to your bed, and wait for the darkness to surround and encompass you. You may find that as you are trying to utilize your day, and build upon the momentum, you might have moments where you want to hide from the world, people, questions, conversations, eyes or difficult feelings of rejection, betrayal, anger and frustration. Initially, the excitement of a new beginning, a new day, ignites hope and desire of opportunity for something different. Then, a memory sparks that reminds you of your loss. It can be a small thing and seem very harmless, such as a smell of someone's cologne, or driving past a former hangout. This is when a shadow of your past relationship and those surrounding emotions cross over your mind, eyes, heart and soul. It may last a minute or it may boomerang you back into the dark overcast of your past for hours or days. In this book you will be given tools to take control of your emotions, rather than letting them take control of you. By taking control of your emotions, you can control the length of time that the shadow lurks. Practice your refocusing and re-centering exercise. Tell yourself, "I am in control." "I am coming back stronger and better than I was before." Shadows will appear, how long they stay, or letting them consume and paralyze you is up to you. You have the strength, the desire and soon you will have more tools to slay the shadows and step back into the light.

In the book, *Walk Two Moons,* by Sharon Creech, a young girl deals with the loss of her mother, and realizes that she is gone and never coming back. Her grandparents, which love to quote funny proverbs, metaphorical idioms and use colorful figurative language, are driving her across the country from Ohio to Idaho, following in her mother's footsteps.

A proverb or idiom is a saying that expresses a truth based on common sense and practical experience of humanity. One of the idioms that the grandparents stated along the journey was, "You can't keep the birds of sadness from flying over your head, but you can keep them from nesting in your hair."

Activity

At this time, turn to the journal pages at the end of this chapter and illustrate a drawing that represents that saying, "You can't keep the birds of sadness from flying over your head, but you can keep them from nesting in your hair." Also, write a paragraph or so next to it explaining what that quote means to you.

What this basically means is, there will be times in our lives that bad things happen. A loss of a loved one through death, divorce, etc. is colossal. We cannot control trials that occur or obstacles that are thrown in our path. Nor can we control the feelings of devastation and intense sadness this experience brings, causing great heartache. However, what we can control is how long we let the heartache capture and hold us captive while time passes us by. Our goal of a new dawn is to break free of the heartache and begin moving in a forward, intentional direction, to become more independent and self-sufficient standing on our own two feet, writing and rewriting a new chapter in our lives. Nevertheless, that does not mean that we are no longer sad at times. We will feel the echoes of anguish from time to time, which I call the shadows that cause a temporary setback and overcast on our upward dreams.

Time and distance will loosen the hold that your emotions have on you, emotions that defeat your strength. This chapter, "Shadows", discusses the shadows that lurk and linger in the corners of your mind and soul. They will cover the light from time to time, but with the right tools, you can lessen the hold the shadows have on you. You will learn how to better control the length of time they cover the light so you can get back to re-writing your new life and future by being able to step back into the light.

Just like the birds of sadness nesting in your hair, it is the length of time we allow the sadness to take up residence and consume our thoughts that affect the ability to break free and begin our forward progress and gain momentum once again. Let the shadows of the past guide your eyes to look up, from the bumps in the road, to the horizon of the future path you want to travel. Truth is the knowledge of things as they are, were and will become. It is unchanging. Stick to truth as your foundation. Truth embraces truth. Light unto light. Truth, courage, strength, gratitude and understanding will illuminate your path moving forward.

Paradigm Mind Shift

As emotions cycle, shadows will return. Instead of letting the shadows define you, have them remind you that without light there is no shadow. If you were standing near a campfire facing the bright, intense heat source in front of you, then you turned 180 degrees around and faced away from the fire, you would be able to see the shadow that your body form created on the landscape before you. As it dances, realize the shadow is formed due to the lack of light moving through a solid object. The light is the energy source, the shadow is the lack thereof. The shadow is the absence of light, hope, energy, warmth etc. It isn't tangible, and you have the ability to control it by making it move or disappear. Realize that the shadow is powerless, it is nothing. It is the absence of the things that make up the light, which are love, energy, warmth, feelings of security, happiness, validity, self-worth etc.

So, when a memory of the past begins to grow within the consciousness of your thoughts, attempting to take control of your emotions and threaten to become larger than what you can handle, realize that you have all the power and control over the shadow and how long it dwells. By shifting your thoughts, you create an intentional movement to turn away from the shadow and turn back to the light of the fire. Search for the source of light to guide your steps away from the shadow containing uncertainty and despair, and shift your thoughts toward gratefulness, appreciation for what you have in this moment and toward the decision to do life differently. The saying, "If you want the same result, keep doing what you have always done." However, I say, if you want a different ending choose to do things differently. That means, keep your focus on the stream of light and move toward re-writing a different result or a future that you want to have. Healing doesn't mean the damage never existed, it means the damage no longer controls your life.

Choose Happiness

One stream of light is hope, and another is gratefulness. In the stillness of reflection, find things in nature you are grateful for. The discoveries of little things that you can say, "In this moment, the cry of a new born baby makes me happy". Perhaps it is the simple sound of birds chirping, or water running down a stream, the rays of sunshine reaching the horizon, or a beautiful flower blooming. You will discover that the item itself isn't making you happy, but the simple act to choose to have an attitude of gratitude for things around you gives you the fortitude to choose happiness. Happiness is a feeling, but if you live an intentional life to be a grateful person, that takes choice and effort. With repetitive decisions to be grateful, it then becomes a way of life. Then one moment builds upon another until you have several moments strung together that you can feel happy and thankful for life. This gift is the beginning of a new day, a new chapter in your life. Adorning the safety jacket that states you are choosing to preserve your life and live it with caution, yet choose to live it. In the beginning, sadness may have consumed your being and your time. Then as light crept in, there were moments you were grateful and happy instead of sad and lonely. Expand on the light by building upon the positive and grateful mind shift to choose happiness.

As the day stretches on, so does your time without tears and grief. I remember going from crying my entire waking hours, to just several times a day. I longed for the day that I would make it a whole day without tears, and finally one day I achieved it. For each grieving person, this is a different amount of time. No one can rush you, including yourself. There are no replacements, pills, people, activities etc. that can keep you from going through the grieving process. You must grieve, including going through the steps of anger, denial, and sadness to reach healing.

Anger is a real and powerful source for calling the shadows to return. There is no doubt that you were hurt, perhaps deceived and wronged along the way. Find a friend or counselor that can hear your frustrations with guided support. Then, just like the shadows that are created out of the absence of light and are really nothing, so are the feelings of anger you are hanging on to. Release those thoughts and feelings, for they are holding you back. They are what keep you stuck in reverse. Let them go, and breathe a deep, cleansing breaths. Let them loosen their binds and become powerless over you. As you release the negative emotions of anger, resentment, or perhaps hatred, you need to replace these emotions with opposite thoughts and feelings that is meant to draw from the light. You have to think and speak words of caring, love, sacrifice, and gratitude. Remember that gratitude and hope are among the emotions that are the tools to bridge you from one side (darkness) to the other (day).

Shedding the shadows is our goal.

How do you combat the negative feelings that creep back in? Just like in Pandora's Box, we are given tools, like a flashlight that will put a stream of light in the darkest of rooms. Your "flashlight" may be surrounding yourself with caring, supportive people including friends and family that help strengthen you to leap over the hurdles that pop up. Talking fears and disappointments with a confidant or counselor helps thicken your protective armor to be able to slay the shadows when they appear. Having people whom you can be completely honest and transparent with is crucial. It opens up a glimpse of understanding for them on how to support you, and as a result you can keep emotions from bottling up and waring on you.

Another way you can combat the shadows is beginning your day with positive thoughts, reflections and affirmations. This isn't like the old Saturday Night Live sketch where you stand in front of the mirror and repeat the same phrase over and over each day, "I'm smart enough, I'm good enough, and gosh darn it people like me..."

Instead, taking time not only to think through specific things you are grateful for, but the action of writing it down makes a cognitive difference. In the first chapter, I recommended purchasing a journal. It can be a fine leather bound book or a simple notebook. In the previous chapter, I mentioned that writing down thoughts and feelings as you are processing from the old into the new is extremely important. It will be helpful to mind dump on pages, reflect on your emotions and feelings as well as be able to read back through it at a later time. It will also be important to begin and end each day with at least 3 positives thoughts. We have mentioned replacing the negative with positive and this activity will help do that.

Activity

In the morning, reflect on people and opportunities you are grateful for and looking forward to. Being specific with items that you are grateful for helps the upward movement and forward progress.

For example:

1. Today, I have a meeting with a client. I am so grateful to be able to have the opportunity to list their house. It will give me exposure for future buyers and clients as well as give me the opportunity to show off my talents as a stager when getting it ready for the market.

2. Today my daughter showed real maturity when handling herself and her job responsibilities. She worked long hours, yet got back up, out of bed and on the road again for another 12 hour day. I feel pride and joy as I see my children growing up into responsible young adults.

3. I have good, supportive friends. Last night a friend said, "You are so good to me." That rang through my ears and reached in to warm my heart. I want those closest to me to not only know I will treat them well, with respect and care, but I want them to feel it so strongly that they can't help but verbalize it. I know that I am a caring and compassionate person whose first tendencies are to treat others with reciprocating care and dignity. I am an honorable, courageous and grateful woman.

Forgiveness

Being grateful is appreciating people, nature and life. However, a person cannot find the ability to be and live a grateful life if they cannot forgive. Those go hand in hand.

Forgiveness lets go of the hurt and negative emotions, so that gratitude can catapult them forward. The bird is allowed to nest in the hair because that person is holding on to something they cannot forgive. For me, I had trouble forgiving my ex-husband for choosing to throw away our relationship. It wasn't perfect, but we had a lot of great times together. I felt I was a pretty good catch, "all that and the bag of chips", and it questioned my belief in myself that he would throw that away to seek it elsewhere. For those where their spouse has passed away, perhaps they are angry at the person for dying or leaving. Or they are angry at God for taking that person from them. I know that I was mad at God for a long time. Somehow part of my being stuck, was being mad that I felt he had lead me into a relationship that failed, and that I got deeply hurt by. To become unstuck, you have to find what pain you are holding on to, that is the bird of sadness, and the only way to let it fly away is to forgive. Once you have done that, you are ready to live a happier life filled with gratefulness and joy.

From that point, I can't think of a better way to shed the shadows of guilt, doubt, pain, and sorrow than replacing those thoughts and feelings with being grateful. I remember in the early months after my separation and divorce, and a friend mentioned that she could still see that pain and sadness in my eyes even though I looked like I had my act together on the outside. I was still a bit bitter and resentful over the actions that lead up to and occurred prior to the divorce. A friend suggested that I pray for my ex-husband. I couldn't even fathom praying for someone that had hurt me so deeply. I looked right into her eyes and said that I was not ready nor in a place to do that. That was because I wasn't ready to forgive him.

After a great deal of reflection, I began to write in an additional journal in which I wrote about things I was grateful for in our experiences together or things he had done during our relationship that I appreciated.

For example, one story I wrote about was the time we decided to take his two boys and my two older kids, up to Box Canyon outside of Twin Falls, Idaho. We had decided to stay the night in a campground near the hot springs we were planning to swim at. The campground was full, all except two "small cabins" that did not contain their own bathrooms or kitchens. I said it would be alright since we would be near the campground restrooms and showers. When we drove past all of the beautiful and already rented cabins in the lot, and drove up to our "cabin", it was such a letdown. They weren't cabins, they were makeshift sheds made out of storage boxes and plywood. I was shocked and didn't know what to say to my kids and new family. I feared the response I might get. Before any of the kids had a chance to utter a word, my (now ex-husband) said, "What a creative dwelling. It is our Chateau Chabin!" with a French accent that broke all tension and lead the way to a positive attitude that turned the situation around and made the weekend a great experience.

Another appreciation was the time and effort that my (ex) husband put into ordering a custom designed engagement ring with a beautiful diamond in the center with a pair of lovely rubies on each side. I loved wearing the ring. It was beautiful and thoughtfully chosen.

The list goes on and on. Over time, my heart began to change from feelings of anguish, resentment, anger etc. to appreciation, love and fond memories that I cherished. I wrote about lessons I learned about myself and ways that I grew as an individual, mother, wife and step mother. It wasn't until I took the time to write these stories and cherished memories in my journal for which I was grateful, that I realized that my mind and soul became "unstuck" from being in reverse as the song in the foreword mentioned.

Giving the Gift of Gratitude

It isn't all about your own life becoming "unstuck". You can write a gratitude journal for another person that will greatly affect and change their life as well. In an earlier chapter we talked about service and turning our thoughts and actions outward toward another person. When we do that we are benefitted as much as the person that received the act of service. The beauty is that you are both touched by the light: love, humility, thankfulness etc. Your acts of kindness toward someone else has a positive and momentous ripple effect.

Here is what I mean. If you remember, I couldn't even act on the advice to pray for my ex-husband during that dark time. Then, when I began making choices to be more positive and grateful I became happier. When I became stronger and began writing down examples I was grateful in my former marriage including my ex-husband and his family, it reminded me that I am a happy person. I am even more happy now that I realize that I am a different person from my experiences, the challenges that I have overcome, and the lessons that I have learned from it. I am also a better, stronger person now than even during the marriage.

The kicker was, when the time came that I gave my gratitude journal to him. I had not spoken to him since the separation and now I show up with a gratitude journal filled with stories and specific things I was grateful for about him. That was both easy and difficult to do. On one hand, it was difficult because I had already given up a lot and he had taken a lot from me including my home, money, pride, happiness etc. However, I had learned to find my own happiness, make my own happiness and live life without him. When a person is truly happy and unstuck, their happiness grows when they share that happiness with others. So, I was a little nervous, but excited to give him the journal. I was at peace with knowing whatever he did with it or thought of it was not a reflection of me, the gift was given.

A period of time later, he contacted me and we spoke about the gift. He said he couldn't believe the depths of forgiveness I had shown by writing and giving the gift. As a result, he had a mind shift, a paradigm shift he called it, that rippled through his personal life and affected his family. He took the act of being grateful and the journal and started one for his two boys, and he said it had improved their relationship. That the same had happened with students and colleagues as work. By my selfless act of gratitude, the ripple effects reached others and made a difference in their lives. Now, our relationship has changed, and when we interact it is from a standpoint of friends. When my grandmother passed away, he was one of the first people to reach out and send condolences. At times he will send pictures of his sons and their accomplishments.

Gratefulness for the experiences we have that make us a stronger, more aware individual, and find appreciation for even the people that have hurt us in the past, flames our light and increases our ability to forgive and love. It is not the mistake or trial in life that we need to center our thoughts and life around, it is the lesson learned. What we do with the new knowledge and how we choose to live our life going forward makes all the difference. It is what defines our character. Helping others, forgiveness, and improving relationships enhances our lives and the lives of others in a positive way. This is a significant turning point in rewriting your future for a better life.

When I was 10 years old, and in the 4th grade I remember my grandfather suddenly passing away. I don't know if there were other funerals of family members I had missed due to my young age, but my father's father was the first funeral I remember attending. The program that was handed out to those attending the service, had a sky with clouds on the front cover. There was no sun, though you knew it was there partly because the sky was all lit up. Also because this beautiful white light lined the outside of the group of clouds casting shadows in its path. It was the evidence of the sunlight, hidden and obstructed by the cloud, but it was there never-the-less. Call it faith or evidence that the light was still there, but I knew at that moment that in spite of a sad situation, your eyes will search for the light. As soon as you find evidence of it, your faith, hope and humility follows, casting away the shadows in your mind.

Let the shadows of the past fade. They are a result from experiences that have affected you, but they do not control you. They are gentle reminders that you are a stronger, different and more experienced person that has the ability to see bumps in the road, and use them to see the horizon of the future path you want to travel.

Once again, truth is the knowledge of things as they are, were and will become. It is unchanging. Stick to truth as your foundation. Truth embraces truth. Light unto light. Truth, courage, strength, forgiveness, gratitude and understanding illuminate your path moving forward. As emotions cycle, shadows will return. Instead of letting the shadows define you, have them remind you that without light there is no shadow. Search for the source of light to guide your steps.

Speaking and writing your thoughts down helps heal the mind, heart and soul. It is ok that you miss this person and that you loved spending time and making memories with. Once you can write those things down, the healing first comes from the truth, being honest about your feelings. Then healing comes from the appreciation of the things you learned from this experience and the gratitude for having the opportunity to use those experiences when rebuilding the new life, new chapter, new future, new you. Remember the phrase, "Healing is not saying the damage never existed, it is saying that it no longer controls your life." At any given moment, you have the power to say, "This is not how the story is going to end," and choose to do things differently, see things differently and re-write your future. The story's ending is not set, it can be changed. It begins with letting in the light and letting your light shine for others.

Activity

In the journal pages at the end of this chapter, take a few minutes right now to write down the following:

1. List a person or persons that you have or are still angry with.
2. What are you angry about, and why are you still angry with them?
3. What do you need to forgive them for?
4. When you are ready, what does forgiveness look like to you?
5. Write down steps you will have to take to get you ready to forgive.
6. Begin the first step.

Perseverance

You must have perseverance and endurance in life to be resilient to the ups and downs and to push away the shadows. The perseverance to endure those ups and downs and enjoy life reminds me of running a marathon.

A number of years ago, I trained and ran a marathon with my running partner that had set a goal to run a marathon for her 50th birthday. This was a time in my life that I got up very early to train, and visit with a gal that was very goal driven and an inspiration to me. After a few short months of training, I was not ready for the race. I had only been training about three months. My times weren't very good, but what I focused on was the end result, finishing the race. To tell you the truth, I think the pace car hit me in my backside more than once. They were anticipating me quitting along the way, but I never quit nor gave up. I just kept a steady pace like the tortious in the story of *The Tortoise and the Hare*.

Somewhere along the way, I caught up with race participants that had run ahead of me in the beginning, whom now were walking and contemplating quitting. I could identify that one girl in particular had hit a wall both physically and mentally. As I kept running, I came into the town with about 6 miles left to go. I had blisters upon blisters. The muscles in my legs were so atrophied that I could not sit down nor lift my leg for the side road medics to place a Band-Aid on my blisters. I couldn't take off my shoes to do it either, so I just kept running. Stepping up on a city curb was a feat on its own. Looking at the cool running water in the ditch along the road looked enticing, but I knew I probably wouldn't climb out of the water filled ditch if I got in it, and would be difficult to find, so I just kept on running. As I jogged down a main street in town, there were participants' family members and towns folk standing on the side of the road clapping, cheering and shouting out words of encouragement. It was then that I hit the wall and with tears streaming down my face out of the overwhelming appreciation for these strangers to clap and encourage me, a stranger, was phenomenal to me. By the time I crossed the finish line, out of 10,000 race participants less than 2,000 finished the race. I was one of them.

I learned a couple of things that day and since that

race. First, it was difficult and grueling at times, but I found the strength to overcome fears, pain and exhaustion to reach my goal. To this day, I say "I have run a marathon, I can handle this." when something challenging comes up. Perseverance in all aspects of life including during dark and difficult times is key to survival. When there are bumps in the road, I tell myself "I can handle it, I have run a marathon." However, it is finding the endurance and the character traits deep down that give us the perseverance to keep going until we make it on the other side.

Second, once you have been through it, hindsight gives great perspective that you can use the next time around or as advice for other people. Besides the regular suggestions of a training plan in preparation for the race, I am referring to things to consider during the race to help you be successful. These include some of the following:

1. Wear the right clothing and supportive shoes (arm yourself with proper tools to be successful in life)

2. Carry your own nutrition when you become calorie deficient (take time to feed your mind, body and soul. Make time to do things that bring you back into balance to avoid deficiency)

3. Get enough sleep and proper nutrition and water intake leading into the race (and in life, these things give us physical strength that supports our mental health as well, including combatting stress)

4. During the race, make friends and enjoy the journey. It makes the 26.2 miles a much more pleasant experience and the time and miles pass by quicker (enjoy the journey of life, making friends along the way)

5. Stop at the water stations and hydrate every mile or

so. It will be a difference maker in your final miles and your recovery (Stop and re-center and re-focus from time to time)

6. Utilize the check in points and medic stations. They have people trained and waiting to assist you and help you be successful in finishing the race. (Lean on the people in your inner circle as needed. Remember to reciprocate, so that you support each other)

7. Keep your eye on your goal and except nothing less (Focus, drive, ambition fuels our initiative to thrive and build better life and a stronger future)

8. If someone needs your help along the way, people are more important than your race times to qualify for the next big race. Prioritize, and keep the big stuff in check and don't sweat the small stuff. (It's a people helping people world. Your life is enriched when you help and serve others. In the course of a lifetime, realize what matters and make sure to give it and the people the attention they need)

These are a few things I learned in my experience. The physical, emotional and mental challenge of running 26.2 miles is very similar to facing the challenges and curve balls that come up in life. They will be easier to manage when our health is good, when we have a knowledgeable and supportive team around us, when we have a game plan in place and we keep our focus on the goal, without sweating the small stuff or the things we cannot change. More of these suggestions can be found as tools for your handbag in the last chapter *of The Unwritten You: Rewriting Your Future.*

In the journal pages at the end of this chapter, out of the eight items of advice for marathon runner and life, which one have you used in your healing? Give an example in your journal. Which one is more difficult to do? Write a paragraph or more, why you might find that item of advice more difficult.

Shadows; The reality is that you will probably see shadows forever. They may be small, and they may be infrequent, but you will experience the loss of loved one or relationship. Take comfort that you will learn to live with seeing those shadows. You will heal and rebuild yourself inspite of them. You will also become whole again, but you will never be the same, nor should you be the same; nor would you want to. Let the shadows and absence of the shadows remind you of the lessons you have learned from your past, and reveal to you that you are not the same person. You have rebuilt yourself, you are stronger and grow happier each day as you rewrite your tomorrow.

Shadows

Date ______________

Date ___________

Date ____________

Chapter Four

Seize the Day

Courage Built Into Action: "Strength doesn't come from doing the things you know you can do; Strength comes from overcoming the things you once thought you couldn't do."

When happy in your relationship, you were loved and supported. Work was going well and it was easy to be positive and productive. When the darkness hit and you were alone and felt directionless, being and staying positive was a challenge. Your greatest growth as a person comes from experiencing difficult times and passing through them a stronger and better individual as a result. Being knocked down happens, it's making a decision to get up, start over, move forward and try again that defines us.

Starting over and seizing the day takes courage; capitalizing on opportunity is putting courage into action. Remember, you must find your passion and drive to give you the strength to rewrite your future. Then, accept where you are, take responsibility for your part in getting yourself to that place and then exercise your courage to change it. Take control of your life and begin re-writing it day by day, page by page. Time is a healer of wounds, and a counselor, but it is you that will have to push yourself to improve each day spiritually, emotionally, physically and mentally.

Activity

At the end of each day, in your journal, reflect how you left your day better than you found it. List:

1. Tasks you accomplished
2. Decisions made that you stand by and are proud of
3. Something you learned that day
4. Words that gave you a renewed hope, ignited drive and pressed you forward.

This writing is just as essential as the transparent writing about the shadows, thoughts, fears and concerns, because you are learning to replace the limiting effects of these negative emotions, and discover you are becoming a new, stronger you through the positive affirmations and journal documentation of your improvements. Use the paradigm shift in thinking to be your own agent of change. Think, speak, write, act to transform into a new way of life that is happier and more fulfilling than the old life.

What is your purpose in Life? Figure out your purpose. If you can't figure out your purpose, then begin with figuring out your passion. Your mind, body and spirit at their core all know what your purpose is, but sometimes it is difficult to realize it. So begin with what you are passionate about.

Ask yourself: What makes you happy just doing it and being in the moment? Is it helping people, teaching people, showing other's the path to independent self-sufficiency? Whatever it is should show up in either your work day or in your hobbies. Identifying your passion and what you enjoy being involved in, will lead you to your purpose.

Keep in mind that your past does not determine who you are, rather your past prepares you for who you are to become. We can gain a different mindset when it comes to our past. Look at your past, as through a student's eyes that learns from these experiences, not a victim of the past that is always looking over his/her shoulder, creating excuses for whey they are "stuck" in life. The truth is, we will never be completely released from our memories and experiences. We will always remember them with joy, sorrow, determination and disappointment. However, with time, the sting of difficult feelings dims and the optimistic light of a new and better future grows. The key to the timing of that change begins with our thoughts and mindset. It goes back to being complacent in a comfort zone of sorrow, like becoming comfortable with that bird of sadness nesting in our hair, or choosing to climb out of your pile of stink, shed the shadows, shoo the birds and walk into the light. Don't let that bird of sadness or that shadow become a well-known friend. It's time to evict them. They are sucking the life out of you. It is time to kick them out.

Look forward, let the rays of light and a love for yourself guide your path. Surround yourself with people that also like to walk in the light that will give you a hand up when you need it. Out of your experience of grief, you may see shades and hues you might not otherwise have seen, but you have to decide and take action to move out of the darkness toward light to see and appreciate the new color.

The new color that I discovered came from passing through the dark and into the light of enlightenment from, and only from, the experience of my divorce. I didn't realize the value and effects of sharing my experiences with others that are also going through a divorce or death of a loved one, until I reached the acceptance stage. When I stepped into the light, after shedding my shadows, I could see the beautiful hues of color of opportunity to share, understand what others were going through and prepare for whom I would become.

Activity

Use paints, chalk, markers etc to draw a dawn, or a horizon, a sunset, or a rainbow etc on a journal page at the end of this chapter. What color do you identify with? How does a color make your feel? Has that color changed since before the event? If so, how or why do you think so? What colors are included in the new hue or shade? Can you think of examples where you have noticed this color more often? Do different colors represent you differently throughout the day?

There is a lot of research on the meaning behind color. What color represents the one you identify with? Peruse the internet to find information about some of the colors you have included. Pay close attention to the mood they represent. Look for colors that are uplifting. Journal your thoughts and what you discovered about color.

Change

One bad chapter doesn't define the rest of your story. The 5 step grieving process takes everyone a different amount of time to bridge through. Each individual must experience Sadness, Anger, Denial, and Isolation (sometimes bargaining) before reaching Acceptance. It is important to experience the emotions of these different phases. If we stay in denial too long to avoid sadness and grieving we won't move forward. Neither will the person that chooses an angry, resentful life. I remember identifying with the stage of isolation when I didn't want anyone to see me sad, weak, lonely etc. It was easier to isolate and cocoon myself from the world, including friends and family, then it was to deal with it. Reach out or let people reach out to you and connect.

Especially ones that are supportive and positive. Avoid people that are negative, complain, play the victim role and that seem to stay stuck in misery. Avoid vices that keep you isolated such as alcohol, prescription drugs or intangible things such as the masks you wear to avoid showing real emotion.

Activity

Use the journal pages at the end of this chapter for the next exercise.

1. Write down the words that come to mind when you went through or are still existing in one of the stages of the grieving process. Or, what you remember feeling during the anger, depressed or isolated stages such as:

   Helpless, disappointment, anger, fear, self-doubt etc.

2. Now, cross out each word and above it write its antonym. For example, for anger replace it with joy. In place of helpless write self-sufficient and above self-doubt write determined. Above afraid replace it with confident etc. Whatever opposite word you can come up with write it down. This is another tool to help you clean-up and clear out negative thoughts still lurking and floating around in your head. Focus on the positives and in each situation that you start to look through the rearview mirror, and readjust to looking forward out the front window and admire the view.

3. Changing the words, are a beginning. It is time to attach a positive, forward moving, intentional action. Start with your breathing exercise. Breathe in the positive word on your list and exhale its antonym.

4. Write down an example in your life where you reflect

and demonstrate that positive word.

One way that I turned my negative words of "scared, insecure, angry etc" to positive words of strong, secure and confident happened during my separation and divorce when I ran into an old friend and school mate. One that had been in my fourth grade class all the way through graduating high school. The last time we had seen each other was when he and his wife's band played at my wedding. After spending a few minutes catching up and relaying the bombshell of the upcoming completion of the divorce, I asked him what he was up to. He mentioned working with a trainer for a self-defense course. He had been working on it for a couple of years, accomplished a few levels of certification and now assists with a women's self-defense class and invited me to come check it out. The next class was the following evening. I had to fight the evening traffic while driving to the next town to find the little house where the class was being held. It turned out it was instructor night, when all the instructors got together to spar and work on moves and hone their teaching skills. I was intimidated, being my first day, and settled on remaining an observer for the evening. It wasn't long and they had me on my feet participating. My years of aerobic training and fitness instructor kicked in and I held my own as I was partnered up for the demonstrations and exercises.

The next week I returned and continued building knowledge, strength and feelings of empowerment if the time came to protect myself. I remember one time where other friends and family members were able to join us, and I was hitting the padded gloves of my partner with a back handed hit combination. It was so loud and strong that unknowingly I was drawing attention to myself. The rest of the participants in the room heard my punches, like cracks of thunder, and stopped to watch and listen. After a few minutes, I became self-aware of being the center of attention and brought my actions to a halt. As the others stared motionless at me, I broke the ice by saying, "I obviously have a little pent up aggression I am working off." The others in the room burst out laughing, because they knew the back history of the pending divorce and could understand the need to release pent up emotions through powerful kicks and hits in a controlled environment. What a great, healthy outlet for me to release these emotions. I looked forward to this class every week. I walked away with working off the difficult feelings in an active, yet therapeutic way, and replaced them with feelings of strength, accomplishment and empowerment.

The theory of motion states that an object in motion tends to stay in motion and an object at rest tends to stay at rest. Our bodies are meant to move. Exercise will help you feel better and enable you to combat the shadows and refocus your redetermination and ignite forward movement once again. Be in motion: take a walk daily, or go to the gym, take a self-defense class, go for a run or a bike ride. Take the opportunity to admire the beauty of nature around you and as you get your heart rate up, and take deeper breaths. Exhale the negative words, thoughts and feelings with the carbon dioxide, and breath in ambition, determination, self-confidence and positive words and thoughts with new breaths of oxygen.

Your mind, like your body must move and be active to seize the day. Reading a good book will show you ways to be a better parent, friend, business person or a better person is very important. Take a college or community class. Remember the whirlpool that had me stuck and strapped to the bottom no matter how hard I pulled and fought against it? The answer was to open my mind to another path, another direction and another way of thinking. Exactly! Another way of thinking is key. Taking time each day to write down what you are thankful for, appreciating what you have is changing your thinking.

Shed the shadows by replacing negative thoughts with more positive ones. Then move your mind and body to create action to change the result. You are worth this new opportunity, this new future. Gaining a new knowledge, reading a personal development book taking classes or attaining a certification to do something different is the beginning of seizing The Unwritten You.

Activity

Look up a topic that you would like to learn more about. This will be a nonfiction source. For example, look up and listen to and watch how to grow your own hydroponics garden, or learning to speak a foreign language, or developing leadership skills, or how to start up your own business. Whatever it is, find a youtube video, podcast, etc that is from a professional, credible and well put together source. Write down the information that stands out to you. List action steps that may go along with the video in your journal pages. Incorporate sound advice that will develop that interest or talent and as a result improve your life.

Seizing the Day Comes from Inspiring Others

Part of the new color and hue, over time, was the discovery that I wanted to take that self-defense training and bring it to other single women, especially those post-divorce or healing from loss of a spouse. My passion was to share the strength in value, character and self-esteem that developed in these self-defense classes. I knew that my passion was to reach out to other women going through similar circumstances, as I was, and help them become stronger physically, emotionally and mentally. This was where my passion and my purpose emerged and the decision to write this book was born.

Once, my 22 year old son was asked to say what he thought his mom's gift to others was. He had benefited from other mom's examples of nurturing, gift giving, advice giving etc. in college with care packages. After a few moments, he answered, "You have the gift of helping people become independent and self-sufficient." Then he went on to give an example of being four years old with me by his side encouraging him to step up on a stool to help load the clothes washer and turn the buttons to begin the wash cycle. He got a laugh from his story, but it is true. I spent over 20 years in the local school district teaching junior high students to be independent thinkers and love learning. I wanted my own children to have that gift as well, starting at a young age. Whether four years old, fourteen or fourty-four, my passion remains the same, to help them believe in themselves, empower themselves through knowledge, and have the strength and endurance to rely on themselves and achieve their goals.

Seizing the Day Comes from Helping Others

The passion to help other women, just like me, realize their inner strength, build on those strengths and grow from life's lessons into something greater is still there. My hope for you is that you discover this for yourself. As you grow and change, you are walking in light. When you have the desire to help others in that similar situation, to learn to slay their own darkness and shed their own shadows, you may be able to take their hand and help them step into the light. This is when you make even bigger strides forward, because you are taking the focus off yourself and helping others and have the opportunity to grow. As a result you have answered your question of what your purpose is.

Activity

Many people think of community service such as volunteering at the local food bank, hospital, or rescue mission, etc. Any and all service has the ability to help you heal. At first, you realize that your problems are small and much less significant in comparison to those around you such as watching a mother agonize over a critically sick child in a hospital, or visiting and serving those in a woman and children's shelter. In serving others, we are humbled to once again gain perspective of all that we have and all we are capable of accomplishing. Acts of service may be as small and simple or large and time consuming. At the end of this chapter, list one person you interact with regularly. After deciding who that is, create a plan of service and execute the plan. Record in your journal whom you gave service to, their reaction, your feelings surrounding the event and the result. Watch the ripple affect as people pay it forward.

Imagine a person that has a rough start to their day. Perhaps they got up late, therefore ran out the door late for work. Since they were hurrying to get to work, they didn't see the police officer before he pulled up behind them and gave them a ticket. From there, this person was in a bad mood the rest of the day and affected all those they worked with. One of those people he worked with went home grouchy as a result and was short with his family member. This is an unfortunate negative sequence of events that can also result in a ripple effect.

On the flip side, what if you were the person that began with a positive attitude as you wrote in your journal reflecting on your day. As a result of your positive attitude, you greeted others with a friendly hello, a smile or even secretly bought the coffee for the person standing in line behind you at the coffee shop. What if you were able to see the positive, rippling effects your actions made as each of these individuals paid that positive action forward? What if you were told that your positive attitude and helpful nature to others made a difference in 10 strangers' lives that day, or 1,000 people's lives that week or 1 million lives for the better over the course of 90 days? Would that make a difference in the small simple acts of being kind or reaching out and helping a fellow man?

Go back to the saying of, "Your past does not determine who you are. Your past prepares you for who you are to become." Go back to your exercise where you replaced negative words and feelings with positives. The next exercise is to brainstorm ways that you can use what you have learned to benefit another person. Begin with writing down your talents. What are you good at? Do you play the piano, are you a good speaker, can you cook or make a mean batch of bread? Share this with others. Your past does not determine who you are, that is true, unless you did not learn nor grow from your experience. Choosing to be more perceptive of others and to lend a friendly, helping hand because you are a different person by what you have been through, is how your past prepared you for who you are to become. What does the person you want to become look like, talk like, act like, think like etc.? Start today to be that person. Show it through your actions toward others.

Activity

1. List 10 talents.
2. After reviewing the list, write down ideas of how you can make a difference in someone else's day by sharing one of these talents that you have.

   *It is one thing to think about it and brainstorm it, it is a totally different experience to execute it.

3. Action and Execution: Start with the basics of smiling at others, saying hello, opening a door for someone. Then move into doing things that take more effort or time and talent. As you make a difference with others, and you see the joy you create, you'll realize you gain a gift as well.
4. Reflection: You are a happier person, when the gift of joy is shared by you. It has the power to bring in more light. In this exercise, choose one place that you can and will complete an act of service to help another person, and watch it help you and aid in your own healing.

Here is a wonderful example. There was a gal that grieved over the loss of her best friend in high school that was taken suddenly at an early age. What this gal did was send her friend's parents flowers every year on her friend's birthday. It was a simple gesture, and for eight years she has done this. It was a way to step out of her own grief and bring light to someone else that was also grieving. The parents of this girl could not put into words what it meant to receive the kind offering, not just at the time of the funeral, but every year for the past eight years. It has been a difference maker in getting through the difficulty of losing their daughter, and has brought them joy as well as to the friend who sends the flowers.

Seizing the Day Comes from Taking Action

You can identify people at work, friends, family etc. that want to accomplish something great or improve their physic or self-image, but they are always talking about what they want. "If I were skinnier, I would be happier." "If I had money, I would be able to take that trip to Europe I have always dreamed of taking." The difference between you and these people is action. To change a hope to a reality is about the action steps taken to get there. In this chapter, the word "Seize" is based on an action not a wishful desire. The difference between successful people and the majority is setting goals, creating a plan, visualizing what it looks like to leap through each step and then carry it out. The execution of the plan is key.

You must have habitual time and space to think about what you want to accomplish, then write these things down and brain storm what tools you need to make it happen. Then begin your day with that plan of action in mind for forward motion. Some people need to write down their schedule and plan of action the night before. For them this is a type of "mind dump" that gives them the peace of mind that they are ready for the new day and can sleep better. For me, the early morning hours, before the sun has come up, I like to lay in bed and think through what challenges I have, what events do I need to attend, what is it that I want to accomplish, and how it fits into my time frame and schedule. Then when I have seen how the day plays out in my mind, I sit up, turn the light on and begin my task list, my plan of attack.

In the book, *The One Thing*, by Gary Keller and Jay Papasan, it encourages its readers to make a short daily task list, identify which task is the most important, then move it to the top. The idea is to complete that task, using all your focus and drive, and then after that the rest is icing on the cake because the most important task has been accomplished. There are also advantages to setting a number of doable tasks in the day, such as 10 tasks. If you write down too many items, it may seem admirable yet as you find yourself rolling many of the tasks into the next day it can instill a feeling of disappointment and defeat rather than success and accomplishment. So, perhaps if you first make 'a short list of high importance items, and then a short list of lesser important items, you can categorized your task list of imminent task to accomplish first.

Take this moment to go to the pages at the end of this chapter and write down the top 10 tasks that need accomplished today. Which of those represent business and provides financial stability? Those would be pretty important because they support your cost of living. Answer which one thing is most important and do that first. Then you can categorize your physical, spiritual, emotional and mental goals and write a task list for those. Make sure you balance your time from work, self and loved ones. Which ones stir your creative drive or hobbies? These will give you a happy balance to the first ones.

Another important action to accomplishing tasks that need done and help you be successful is to identify what part of the day are you most optimistic, energetic and clear, and do those important items at that time. For example, many people, after a good night's rest and their cup of Joe, feel more strong minded and can manage even the problem solving tasks. Whereas, if they try to take care of a large project in the afternoon their feelings of procrastination and fatigue creep in, which allow insecurities to put off the task till the next day. Some people like to get up, take a run or get in a workout in that gets their focus and creative juices flowing, get something to eat and then they are ready to tackle the big items late morning to midafternoon. Others get into their groove in the late evening hours. It doesn't really matter as long as you reflect on which hours of the day are you more productive, and then tackle the list of action items during those hours.

Procrastination not only puts progress on hold, but it also sets goals back days and weeks. For most entrepreneurs, they will tell you that taking immediate action on an item gets the deal, makes the progress, and is the difference maker. The law of motion is that an object in motion stays in motion and an item at rest stays at rest. So if you have the ball rolling, it is easier to keep it rolling. If you stop, take a sabbatical or hiatus emotionally and physically after a tragic event like you have been through, it takes more time and effort to get moving in a forward direction again. Each day, you have to consciously and intentionally take steps forward.

Another way to aid you in having the tenacity to take action is to make sure you get enough rest. In the last chapter of this book, "Be-Do-Have" I will expand on making healthy choices that includes rest. Basically, getting enough rest will help you have the strength to endure and avoid procrastination in order to take action and seize the day. You need at least 7-8 hours or rest each night, and not just any 7-8 hours. It is important to start going to bed the earlier. The saying, "Early to bed, early to rise, makes a man healthy, wealthy and wise," has some truth to it. It is difficult to be productive if you are groggy from lack of sleep and you don't feel like being productive. So, the first step is to make it a priority to get to bed early and receive a minimum of 7-8 hours of rest. Then, when your alarm goes off you are ready to jump up, get moving and seize your day. There is research and documented data that shows that if you don't get enough rest and you make it a habit to hit the snooze button over and over, this procrastinating creates a habit that you carry throughout your day. Instead, make a goal to get up and begin taking action on the first sound of your alarm. Or better yet, get enough sleep that you wake up naturally on your own earlier or just before your alarm so you have time to ponder on your day. Train your mindset to develop the drive and determination that begets success, to increase the will to get up and begin moving on it.

Some days are harder than others if the shadows have consumed the corners of your mind, or you have let other's words bring you down or let your emotions take control of you. Progress comes to a halt. Time is limited, each day has finite minutes in order to accomplish the things you need to make it a successful day. So, you will need to let your own passion and drive for something better aid you to hear that inner voice that not only wants to make a change, but knows you are capable of making a change. Don't let others thoughts, opinions and stifling comments and words of advice drown out your inner voice. This is your life, your time, and only you can pick yourself up throughout the day, dust yourself off and make the decision to continue to rewrite the unwritten you. Don't give up, never give in, and draw a fist of determination to knock out the obstacles standing in your way. You are worth it. You have a valuable life to live and things to accomplish. If you didn't, then you wouldn't have had these experiences that have leant themselves to such great lessons learned. Reach deep down and find the inner strength and inner voice to make a declaration that you will not go quietly into the night again. Things will be different, you are different and you are not going back. Discover what is your "fight song, take back your life song" and let it feed your initiative.

You were given this life because you are strong enough to live it. For what it is worth, it is never too late to be whomever you want to be. I hope you live a life you and your loved ones can be proud of. If you are finding that for any reason you are not living a life you want, I hope that you have the strength to start over. This book will give you the tools to draw strength that you may not know you had, to not only start over but write your future yourself, as you see fit.

Take a stand, make a declaration. Announce to the public that if they see you based on who you were a year ago, they do not know you at all. Your growth game is strong. It is time to Re-Introduce yourself.

Activity:

I. The next activity can be first written down in the pages at the end of this chapter, but can continue in your separate, daily journal.

Directions:

1. List 10 words that represent you as a new and growing person.

   For example strong, compassionate, caring, honest, successful, achiever, insightful, valiant, beautiful and determined.

   ____

   ____

   ____

   ____

   ____

2. Now sketch a picture that represents what you think of when you imagine yourself, in your new day, seizing the day. Label the objects in the picture.

3. Now take those words and write them by weaving them into your picture. This is a concrete poem and is effective to see you, your day, and your future with these

words at the very fiber of the picture, your image, your vision. You can write the words over and over along the lines of the picture or make the words the picture.

II. Another wonderful type of poem is an acrostic poem. You can see an example here, and then write your own in the journal pages at the end of this chapter.

Directions:

1. Write your name down the length of the page, like this:

   J

   A

   N

   E

   T

2. List adjectives that represent who you are beginning with each letter. It is absolutely ok to list words you would like to become as well. For example:

   Jubilant

   Abundant

   Nurturer

   Encourager

   Tenacious

3. List the definition of each word and an example in your life that you have demonstrated this word.

   Jubilant: joyous, rejoicing.

I rejoice for being alive and the blessings I am given. I am grateful for my life, and I smile a lot reflecting my joyous feelings.

Abundant: abounding, bountiful, plate is full.

It is a joke with my family when someone asks me what I do, that they respond with, "You mean what doesn't she do?" I like to have a full and busy plate. I like investing in others and watching them grow. I like sharing my time and talents with my children and others.

Nurturer: To support and encourage

I have been a teacher and coach for nearly 20 years, supporting the learning of nearly 20,000 students. However, my most important role has been being the nurturer for my own 3 children.

Encourager: To inspire with courage, spirit, or confidence.

This is the bases for writing this book, *The Unwritten You*. It would bring me great satisfaction and joy to know that the words in this book have been a positive influence for someone else.

Tenacious: Origin tenacity: Strong, Unyielding.

I appreciate the times that my children have told me that I am the strongest woman they know. Once I was counseled by my father to be the mortar that holds the family together. Right now that would be my children and me. In the future that may be a combined family mixed with step children. I want them to see me as someone that endures to the end, not a quitter, so showing tenacity or living a tenacious life is important to me.

In conclusion, it takes a lot of drive, determination, action and resilience to seize the day. Chart your daily progress in your journal and identify how much more you get accomplished on a daily basis.

Seize the Day

Date ______________

Date ____________

Date ___________

Chapter Five

Rise and Shine

This is your journey, live an intentional life.

Accept that all your past experiences and life's lessons will always be a part of you, and that you don't need to carry guilt about moving forward. You can find hope, redemption, gratitude and the determination to carry on. Not only live, but to live well. It is time to clean up and clear it out. Wipe the slate, start with a blank paper and begin writing your new chapter.

In Natasha Bedingfield song called "Unwritten", she describes this stage of the journey well. At this point in time, you are unwritten, undefined. This is your beginning, the pen is in poised, and it is up to you from here forward. Your ending is undetermined and unplanned at this point. You have the ability to rewrite your future as if you have a blank page sitting in front of you. Instead of staring at it, in this book you are taking action steps with guided practice and new knowledge to do something productive with it. Let your new sunlight illuminate new words and new vocabulary. Reach for something different, like that plant root or rock, and pull yourself out of the whirlpool and take back control of your life. It is so close you can almost envision it and touch it. Release your doubts, your inhibitions, take risks, take chances and go for it. The time is now, that old world is now a new world for you.

No one else can do it for you, can make the leap of faith and take the steps necessary for change. No one else can think, write, and speak the words of encouragement to yourself like you can. Saturate your day in positive, uplifting words and thoughts each day. You have the strength to live your life with arms wide open, vulnerable, trusting, authentic, transparent and genuine. Today your book begins; tomorrow and beyond is still unwritten.

The future is yours to lose, win, throw away or create. It is up to you. Since you were a little child, teachers, parents, and mentors have told you that your future is yours to be and do anything you put your mind to. You can be anything you want. You can create this future by seeing and following your dreams. Perfection is unattainable, but by reaching for it and exercising your potential, you can attain greatness; if you want it. In the following chapter, I will outline steps on how you can begin to attain the future you have dreamed was possible, but could not understand how to define it, let alone achieve it.

If you view life's events as no accident, then it makes sense to take the perspective that we are students and life is a lesson. If we are willing to pay attention to the lesson we will become transforming, trusting, positive, forward thinking, growing individuals. Change doesn't happen when something is not working, growth comes from taking what we have learned and apply it to our lives. Don't be afraid to take risks, it is where we experience the greatest learning curve. Avoid waiting for a miracle to land at your feet to make you change your reality, it is up to you to make the change happen. You have the ability and the power to change your present circumstances. It takes mindset, planning, action, positive thinking, intentional deliveries, trying and trying again and learning from the experience to inspire growth. Many entrepreneurs failed their way to success. Failure is just our first attempt at learning. It's a numbers game. The more you fail, the closer you are to success. The lesson many times is in trying again and never giving up. Winston Churchill said, " Success is the ability to go from failure to failure without losing your enthusiasm."

No matter what you have gone through and what challenges you face day to day, it is what you do with the lesson learned that matters. The wisdom is in the realization of what isn't working, reflecting, problem solving and sometimes changing courses to create something that does work. Reflect on how you want your day and your life to be. Visualize your day, accomplishing a task, what that leap of faith looks like and you will begin to land on the positive side of things. As negative thoughts and shadows creep into your mind, replace them with positive thought and ideas and you will initiate positive results. Yesterday cannot be recovered, but today is ours to act and accomplish a different result than what you have received thus far. Believe that each day is worth living, be positive and forward thinking, making intentional decisions with a plan of action, and your belief will help create the fact.

Master Your Emotions

As previously mentioned it is important to find your "why"for moving forward. The passion you hold on to, can motivate and inspire you. Some people may tell you not to let your feelings get in the way, to ignore them, because they interfere and hold you back. I disagree in that your feelings are basis of your passion. If you can bridle your feelings to create inspirational goal setting and achieving passion you are stronger and more effective. Your passion is the motivation that helps you pick yourself back up over and over again. Passion challenges failure and forges ahead with a no-quiet attitude, looking for the next opportunity to achieve. Keep your eye on the goal ahead, the light at the end of the tunnel and readjust your action based on lessons learned.

Redirect frustration and defeat into drive and determination. Live life to the fullest by focusing on the positive, and you will more likely live life to the fullest. With an adventurous outlook, attitude and always, consistently giving your best effort, you will eventually tackle the immediate challenges and prepare yourself for greater things. How can you become prepared to tackle immediate challenges? What gives you the admonition to have the strength to pick yourself up after rejection, or the fortitude to make a new plan and execute it, and the clarity of mind to focus on the important things to drive you forward toward success? How do you wake up in the morning, determined to view life today through the windshield rather than the rearview mirror? Well, you have to be strong physically, mentally, spiritually and emotionally.

Here are a few daily choices, if turned into habits, that will get you there.

1. **Choosing a healthy lifestyle.**

In order to feel good, and be the best you can be, you have to start with taking care of yourself on the inside. Nutrition, rest, water intake and exercise are the four components of good health. Let's start with rest. There are a lot of stresses that continue to come at you from all directions. Perhaps it is financial stability and your job that you must keep to pay the bills. Perhaps it is family or other personal relationships. No matter what the stress is, you will be able to handle it better if you are fully rested. This doesn't mean sleep all day to keep from facing the stress, it means getting 7-8 hours consistently each night. Being well rested will help you have the energy and patience for what comes your way. Think of a very cute three year old. They are easy to please, happy, interactive, energetic etc. However, what happens when they are tired and haven't had enough rest? They get irritable, grumpy, and short tempered, and they cry over the littlest things. We do the same thing. The straw that broke the camel's back, is sometimes due to being tired and exhausted. So, remember, that a full night's rest will help battle against the daily stresses that come your way.

Next is nutrition. Research says that 80% of weight goals comes from good nutrition. If you want to lose a few pounds, gain muscle, or just feel better it starts from the inside out. Cut down on alcohol, caffeine, high carbohydrate foods, sugared foods, fried foods processed and high fat foods. Take out, carry out and food from a drive through are not your friend. Try to get back to the basics of eating whole natural foods that you can grow. When sad and emotional, many times people turn to comfort foods. They think, and perhaps it is true, it makes them happy in the moment. It tastes good, it feels good for "A moment on the lips, but it is forever on the hips" I used to hear. Beyond that, when you gain weight it magnificently affects your self-esteem. Processed, sugared and fatty foods don't leave you feeling well in the long run and they wreak havoc on your system, increase the chances of gaining weight and then leave you feeling sad, down, more depressed and weak. On the other hand, healthy foods contribute to you feeling good, strong, healthier, and overall affect your healthy wellbeing. As soon as you begin to look healthier, feel better, and your clothes are fitting better, your outlook of yourself, your future and your potential begins to change for the better. Even in the simplest ways such as people you see saying, "It's good to see you. You look good." Is so different than, "I am so sorry. I can tell this is taking its toll on you." Feeling good about yourself is the first and most important giant leap forward on the journey of rewriting your future and getting there.

Water intake goes hand in hand with good nutrition. Our bodies are made up of mostly water. Water is our life source. You have heard the rule of drinking 8, 8oz glasses of water. Many people think that if they stop by the drinking fountain, that they have had their water intake for the day.

Calculating how many ounces of water you drink is the first step. Begin with the common 64 ounces of water, and once that is mastered and is a habit try to drink more. If you are an active person, spend time outside in the heat, athletic, etc. then you will need to drink more water. Some statistics say to take your body weight, cut it in half and that is how many ounces of water your body needs to function. So for a 160 lb woman she would need to start with 80 ounces. Then if she did the next step of a healthy lifestyle, which is daily exercise, she would need to increase her water intake again. The easy water goal for me, when I am trying to increase my health goals and exercise is to shoot for a gallon of water, and 2 hours of activity.

Leading an active life including daily exercise take more effort to plan into the daily schedule. As times change, young and old find themselves more sedentary...unlike during my mother's growing up years of walking miles to school and upon returning home had to go out in the fields to tend to the farm. My mother and grandmother lead active lives where movement was built in to the family survival and income earning. Today, we sit in a chair at a computer, travel in our car or stand in one place waiting on customers for the most part. We have to be more intentional to build time in our day to be active. Being active two hours a day is optimal. That can be a 45-60 minute walk/run morning or night. An aerobic and active class at the gym, weight training or playing a sport to name a few. When we move our bodies, the endorphins created inspires motivation and change. Have you ever taken a fun zumba class or fitness class at the gym and right afterward you felt great and ready to put a schedule in place to attend classes 3-5 days a week, only to struggle to make excuses and procrastination later? Those are the endorphins.

I experienced a whole gamut of emotions during a local women's fitness run a few years ago. I had set a goal and put a plan in place to be prepared to do well as I worked toward this 5K fall race. During the opening of the event, people were excited for the race, music was playing and the crowd was lead in motivational movements designed to fire up the crowd and warm up the muscles. Then as we moved to the line and waited for the sound of the starting gun to echo through the air I thought to myself, "What am I doing here, I don't really want to do this." Then the race began and I knew I had to follow through. I paced myself and pushed to keep at a timely 7 mile pace or under. Then just as I began to feel the effects of this pace with shortness of breath, a terrible side ache and a nauseous stomach, I saw the light at the end of the tunnel, the finish line in the distance.

A supportive friend tried to run up and take a video of me completing the race, but I barked to turn it off so I would refrain from being sick on camera. As I crossed the line, there was a strong sense of pride of accomplishment. Then as my heart rate regulated and the endorphins flooded my system the lasting thought was, "That was so great. I can't wait to do another race."

2. Be intentional.

Each action needs to be purposeful

In order to redefine who you are and your new future, you must be deliberate and intentional in your decision. You may struggle with what is a right or wrong decision, especially if you are learning to take more risks. Remember, it isn't about right or wrong, it is about if the process is working or not working. Make a decision, try it out for a while to see if it works, and if it doesn't then change your actions and behaviors toward a different directions until it works.

3. Achieve Clarity.

You have to decide what it is you want to accomplish. Just like training for a race if you don't have something you are working for you lose in accountability, timeline of action and goal setting and the sense of achievement. Wrap your mindset around a target, then visualize the steps to get there. Many times you need to imagine how you want the day or event to work out, then work backwards on a timeline of the action steps needed to get there. For example, with my business I sometimes stage houses that are on the market. I visualize every piece of furniture and staging items I need room by room. From there I schedule movers and locations dates etc. Once the items are in the home, I place each piece according to where it fits best. The picture comes together based on the clear vision I had in my mind's eye before I even began.

4. Define desired outcomes.

You must know what you want before you make a plan to get it. What are the desired outcomes you are trying to achieve? Make a list, include cause and effects for your decisions and actions and do the best you can to keep your eye on the target. If you aren't sure what you want, or where you want to go or how to get there no one can help you along a journey with no path. This comes from your purpose, your passion, your core, and is the base for the *Unwritten You.*

Make a list of things you want to accomplish. Cut pictures out of magazines. It can be fitness goals, financial goals or relationship goals. Get your ideas on paper in the form of words, statements, pictures etc.

5. Discover your Core.

Remember who you are, your self-worth, your core. No one can take that from you, and only you can find it, use it, and make it the base of your goals and actions. Who were you born to be, the skills you have to accomplish great things, and who you have in your inner circle as a support system is your equation for success. These are points that must be thought about and reflected upon in order to move forward.

6. Eliminate the negative and accent the positive.

You must begin one-by-one to eliminate negative, drama and unhealthy things or people in your life. If they don't support the goodness at your core, reinforce your self-worth, and cheer you on as you set and accomplish goals you need to decide if they are raising you up or tearing you down. Once that realization has occurred, you must take action on embracing or removing the item or person from your life. For you to rewrite your future into something spectacular, you need all the positives and supportive hands you can get. You just came off of a difficult time period in your life. You are still healing and to have conflict is really draining. One by one, replace negative words, people and circumstances with positive words, people and circumstances. Follow simple action steps to attain new habits, replacing old unhealthy habits. Reflect in your daily journal pages habits that you feel set you back or keep you from reaching your goals. Start with your choices and actions. From there you can connect those choices to people in your circle that are linked to those bad decisions or limiting actions or good productive decisions and actions.

Then reflect on 10 new habits that you can do daily or weekly that will make a difference in the positive, forward movement of your life.

7. Consistency of small simple things over time makes all the difference.

You can't eat the elephant all at once, you have to do it one bite at a time. Each day set your goals, write out an action plan, get your rest, water and good nutrition, remove stress and replace it with positive motivation. Each day, the key is in the consistency. A river cuts through a rock not because of its power, but of its persistence. It takes daily commitment, daily awareness, daily action, daily positive mindset, and daily adjustment and on and on to make it happen. With every positive step and change you become a stronger and more enduring person.

8. Re-define your mission statement.

Just as a business creates a mission statement, so do you. What is your mission? What is your "Why" for doing what you do? Figure that out and you will find your mission. It may be the everyday action and decisions or it may take weeks or months to accomplish. You can have a mission statement for every aspect of your life or one thing you want to accomplish this year. Set short term goals and long term goals and center those on who you are, what you want to accomplish and you will find your mission statement. Write it and post it. Use it for business and your personal life. From your mission statement, which comes from your core values, people will know you. It will build your reputation and your integrity is defined by it. Make sure your core values, mission statement, words, actions and your results are all a match.

9. Tenacity: Never give up.

List 10 words that represent the statement "Never Give Up" to you.

Here are a few to get you started:

1. Strength	6.
2. Determined	7.
3. Consistent	8.
4.	9.
5.	10.

As you rewrite your future each day, take one of these words and own it for the day. Make choices based on what a ________ determined person would do, for example. Write declarative statements surrounding the word that represent you. List examples in your journal how you were strong or determined that day. Those journal entries will help you in days to come and will set a good example for your children. Your children and grandchildren will be able to draw from your examples, your words and the behavior you model.

10. Be aware of who you are being.

Be happy, be appreciative, be supportive, be involved, be truthful, be smart, be still, be humble, be prayerful, be mindful of others, be kinder than necessary. As you are redefining yourself, you are becoming stronger and more determined etc. However, how you treat others along the way will make the longest lasting influence. Years will pass, and people will still remember your kindness. When speaking with others or resolving conflict, remember it isn't as much what you say but how you say it. Your inflection, your tone, your attitude. Patience is a virtue and it will shape many future situations. If you can remember to be patient and kind, and do acts of service for others every day you will heal faster and will create a more abundant future full of supportive people in your inner circle, such as business colleagues, friends, family members etc.

Being kinder than necessary is an interesting process to watch and take note of. You can do this while driving in your car, interacting with people at the grocery store, bank etc. The golden rule still applies to treat others how you want to be treated, which is a pretty good rule to live by. We cannot measure others by our own yard stick but we have a pretty good gauge and sense on how that goes. This all returns to serving others, reciprocation and gratitude once again. In your daily reflection and in your journal list examples of how you were kinder than necessary and the effect it had on others. Make sure to also list examples when you were not and things didn't go so well. That way you can learn from those experiences also.

As a teacher, I see every day how treating others is remembered. Consider how your responses, acts of kindness and their responses shape your reality and make memories. Ten years from now, what will matter? The car you drove or the relationship you have with your child/grandchild?

Activity

Take the opportunity at this moment, to list on the journal pages at the end of this chapter, 10 things that over the course of a lifetime won't matter. A hint is that they will probably be tangible, material things.

Now list 10 things that over a course of a lifetime will matter. This may be how you spoke to your parent or loved one. Actions or choices that you make, etc.

Some of these steps are repetitive from earlier chapters. Take this time to review and reflect some of the highlights and ideas that stood out to you as your read through the chapters. Review how these top 10 items in your handbag will be strategic and effective tools to pull out, think about, use and put into action on a daily basis to make a difference in your life and in the lives around you.

Take this time to turn to the journal pages at the end of this chapter and write down some of the new tools in your handbag that you have decided to use to live an intentional life as you move forward. What are some of the Be-ing that you will implement into your life?

At the graveside service of my 96 year old grandmother, my aunt mentioned some of the characteristics of my grandmother that my aunt was determined to implement in her life. Some of those things included hard working, enduring and determined. Next in your journal, list people that have been influential in your life that exemplified a strong character that you appreciate and would like to be like.

Rise and Shine

Date ____________

Date ___________

Date ______________

Chapter Six

Be+ Do=Have

Accept what is, let go of what was, and have faith in what will be.

"Those whom I have admired for their strength and grace did not get that way because things worked out. They got that way because stuff went wrong and they handled it. They handled it in a thousand different ways on a thousand different days, but they handled it and those people I look up to. They are my heroes." Author unknown.

When rewriting your future, you have to start at the beginning. Reflect on memories from your childhood, growing into your adult years. It is only when you reflect on memories that created feelings of joy, content, happiness, sadness, fear, anger or insecurities that you begin to understand how the beginning of your story influences your story now and the ability to write your future. There are events in relationships and circumstances that create triggers that affect how you anticipate, interpret and react to situations that cross your path.

For example, when I was about five years old, my family took a trip to California. This was a time when you piled parents, grandparents, aunts and uncles, siblings and cousins into a station wagon and took long family road trips. This was a time when seat belts were not required and younger kids sat on laps, on floorboards or all piled in the very back on a mattress where we could play cards sitting criss-cross as we watched the outside scenery fly by. We would play Crazy Eights, Kings

Corners, Rummy, Fish and Old Maid for hours, only getting interrupted with the occasional rest stop break. And when we did stop, there was no question that you utilized this break, because you may not get another chance for another 200 miles.

On one pit stop, we all filed out of the Forest Green 1970 station wagon. Being one of the littlest I was last to climb out, proceed to the rest rooms, wait in line, use the facilities, wash my hands and walk out to climb back into the car once again. Only this time, when I finished washing my hands, and walked out of the woman's restroom it was to my surprise and chagrin to see the Chevy Station Wagon exiting the rest stop and pulling back onto the highway without me! Keep in mind, there were no cell phones so I couldn't just hit speed dial nor use the payphone to alert my parents that they were leaving their third child behind at the rest stop. So, I plopped myself down on the grass and did the only thing I could do, which was wait for them to realize I wasn't in the car and return for me. That was not likely to happen right away. See, when there are that many kids and cousins in the car, with multiple adults with younger ones on laps visiting, quiet middle children aren't addressed that often, so I knew it would take awhile.

However, sometime down the road, out of the blue, as the story was told to me, my mother had a notion to call out my name to check on me and I didn't answer. I am sure everyone in the car was quite surprised to realize I wasn't in attendance, and their hearts sank and their mouths dropped thinking of such a small child left alone several miles back. Anyway, as you can imagine the desperate U-turn my father took through the median and the "pedal to the metal" hustle he put on it to return to the rest stop to find me sitting and visiting with a nice older couple that was keeping me company until their return.

After having the opportunity to reflect on this experience lately and evaluate what effects is had on my current thinking and reaction to situations, I know that I get frustrated when left behind, or not invited along. I take it personally when I feel I am forgotten or overlooked. On the flip side the happiness and validity I feel when someone goes out of their way to invite, include or think of me is also there. Another strong life lesson that has flowed through my life like a steady stream, is the feeling that if I want something in life I have to go out and get it myself. I can't wait on others to do it for me; I am the one I can count on. I am strong, independent and self-sufficient standing on my own two feet. I put myself through college, the only child to graduate and go on to get my master's degree. I have a career of teaching grade school and middle school, I run my own business, I have invested in other businesses and have enjoyed being an ambassador for the Boise Metro Chamber of Commerce, Garden City, Meridian, Idaho and Business Network International, The Grotto Group, member of The Idaho Women Business Owners Association and more. Then in the last couple of years I have enjoyed taking my expertise and experience and sharing it with others as an author and guest speaker. All of this with the same mentality of, I can do this on my own, don't panic, process a solutions, and be content that everything will work out like when I was five.

You have probably heard many people in your life that can't wait for something better to come along. They are tolerating the present, waiting for the one big break that will bring them happiness. For example, parents that have a baby and can't wait until their toddler is potty-trained, or until they stop teething, or get out of the terrible two's, or go to kindergarten, or graduate high school etc. And then, in what seems like a blink of an eye their child is off on their own. They don't get to see them as often, perhaps have a family of their own and career and we wish we could have some of those earlier years back to enjoy. Some parents spent so much time waiting for the next phase that they forget to enjoy the moment, the phase their child was currently in, and it quickly became the past.

When I was in my 20's, I had three wonderful children. Before I knew it, I was a very over weight (nearly 200lb) 28 year old needing to take off multiple years of pregnancy weight. I started off getting back into shape by taking water aerobics at one of the local health clubs. Before long, I was getting certified and teaching classes at multiple health clubs throughout the city. Within a couple of years, I had set my sights on becoming a national water aerobic instructor and teaching classes for the National Fitness Conferences for the Aquatic Exercise Association including writing and publishing articles for their magazine. One of the classes I taught while at their conference in the beautiful Sanibel Island in Florida, as well as internationally to Sydney, Australia for their National Fitness Conference was called, "Enjoying the Journey." The class was based on experience working with participants whether in class or training in the weight room that wanted to be fit now. To lose weight now. That life would be better if they were fit and weighed 20-40 pounds less now. I encouraged them to not wait to be happy when they met their long range goal, but to enjoy the journey and be happy every step of the way. Also, to enjoy the empowerment they experienced when they chose to eat clean, or the friendships they made as they consistently went to class, or the new muscle definition they could see in the mirror as they cut fat and increased their muscle mass.

Life is the journey and it is ours to enjoy even when there are bumps in the road or unexpected detours we didn't anticipate. Happiness is a choice we wake up and make every day, and no matter what happens it is our day to enjoy our journey, rather than want to skip to the end to find satisfaction. Life won't "be better when... we find the end of the rainbow." Life is wonderful dancing in the rain and smelling the washed clean pavement, or rain-drenched flowers. Like the saying, "Yesterday has come and gone and cannot be changed, tomorrow is not a given, but today is called the present because it is our gift to do with it what we want. So make the most of it. Happiness is in the connections we have with others, the sense of accomplishment with new found skills or honed in talents, and living each day with gratitude." Author unknown.

Be

Don't wait for the next perfect moment, take the moment and make it perfect.

How do we take advantage of living in the moment? The key is to "Be here now." Slow down and observe the people you care about and let them know how you value their friendship and their love. It is in the Be-Ing in the moment. Notice the sunrise as it slowly changes from dusk to dawn. Watch the sun light up the mountain tops and give the clouds a bright silver lining. Delight in watching two squirrels chase each other through the tree tops. Take a bite of fresh fruit off the tree or vine, kiss the top of a baby's head, give hugs to people that linger and say, "I am drinking you in and taking in the moment." Take your life on the movie screen that is flying by like the pavement outside that Chevy Station Wagon, and slow it down to reflect on what you have and what you are grateful for. Who do you have in your life that you appreciate and would be devastated if they weren't with you tomorrow? Let them know what you love and admire about them today, for tomorrow has no guarantees.

You must first reflect on who you are, what you value and what personality traits you want to be known for and project in the universe. The initial step to rewriting your future is to come to know yourself, at your core, and who you want to be: seen as, known as, and remembered as. That is where you find joy, initially. From there, is the "Do" portion. You take what you have discovered about yourself, influenced all the way back to the beginning and growing up. Use the lessons learned, and draw strength to develop skills that you need to write the future you want to have. There is a sure recipe of strength, determination, confidence, happiness, choice, accountability, gratitude and a touch of sassy attitude that will carry you through events, trials, ups and downs, unexpected detours, hurdles and break-throughs.

Do

Don't downgrade your dreams just to fit your reality, upgrade your commitment and perseverance to match your destiny.

Have the fortitude to make decisions and own them. Be determined to follow through, own the consequences, and evaluate what is working and not working and be flexible to adjust as necessary. Those that let time go by, wishing for something different or better never achieve it because they are waiting for it to come to them. They may also complain about the things that always happen to them. Successful people, true entrepreneurs do spend time visualizing what they want. However, it is the action step of setting and writing down the goals that begins to set those two characters apart. The major step is the action step to follow and achieve the goals through movement, action, doing. Nothing changes unless you change, it begins with you. You can't wait for opportunities to fall in your lap, go look for them. Unsuccessful people complain about the things that happen to them and focus on their bad luck. This is a passive excuse for not taking the initiative to change their present circumstances and make a decision to move out of it, into the light and in a forward motion to something different. Change is hard for many people, it is uncomfortable and outside their realm of their comfort zone. Also, for the non risk takers, if they aren't the one responsible for the decision, then they are not at fault for the consequences. Remember, nothing grows inside the comfort zone and nothing spectacular nor great is a by product of the comfort zone. Take a risk and step out of your comfort zone and take a look around. You will find that stepping outside of it gives you room to grow and expand your wings.

Point of View Change Activity

Directions for Point of View Change Activity

Point of view is the angle or perspective from which a story is told. In this activity, you will be rewriting statements to 1st person point of view using the pronoun "I".

1. Please rewrite the following statement at the top of one of your journal pages at the end of this chapter. "If you want a different result, you have to change the way you are doing things."

2. Now rewrite the statement using (I) instead of (you). Example: "If I want a different result, I have to change the way I am doing things."

3. After rewriting the statement in 1st person, continue by writing a paragraph of what that statement now means to you. Do you feel the ownership of that statement and the ability to take control, change or shift in some way? If so, how? Explain.

4. Do the same point of view change for other statements found in this chapter and other chapters as you are reading. Write them in your journal in 1st person. Notice how empowering it is to mentally, emotionally

and then physically take control of your thoughts, actions, decisions and destiny.

If you want a different result, you have to change the way you are doing it. If you are constantly doing things the way they have always been done, you will continue to get the same result. This book is about feeling the fear and take a step forward anyway. Take a risk, put a dream into action. Make a dream board. Write your goals down. Talk about them with others. Put up pictures and affirmations to remind you of your goals and what you want to achieve. Figure out your "why" and you will find your passion. Be grateful for what you have, but always want more. Don't settle. Learn from failures, they are the first step to learning and growing and figuring out what works and what doesn't so you can do them differently the next time until you achieve success. The lesson is found when reflecting on what didn't work, the growth is when you pick yourself up and try again and again and again until it works.

Plan ahead. You are not the mouse in the maze that runs around aimlessly. Pull back and take a look at the puzzle. Imagine the routes that might work to solve the question and resolve any problems that might come up. Envision problems that might arise and possible solutions so that when a road block appears you have the level head to take a different route and the ease of flexibility to change directions when necessary. Have a plan B in case the first plan doesn't work out. If you always have another plan, then you will always have the answer to. "What do I do next?" Put together a game plan and a materials list needed to accomplish the task ahead of time. The less you fly by the seat of your pants, the more prepared you will be and prepared to handle what comes your way.

Figure out what skill set you will need to accomplish your goals. If you don't have the skill set will you set out to acquire them? Will you find responsible, reliable people that have what you lack and delegate? These are questions you process at the beginning of your day and then reflect and evaluate at the end of your day. You may need to enroll in some classes or certify on line to get equipped for what you want to do. Many people, especially women, when left single after a divorce or being widowed are found lacking the skill set to get a job or a higher paying job to support their household on their own. If I could give others some good advice, it would be to think ahead and get set out on a course to be qualified for that job before they find themselves in that position. However, we know that hindsight is 20-20, so we can see how important it is that we are ready to step into a position to be sole provider if we have to. If we or a friend wasn't ready for that, how do you answer their question of "What do I do now?"

Brainstorm and discover what you are good at. Can you teach that skill to someone else? Can you fill a need that a customer base or the community needs filled? It may be the knowledge of quilting, gardening or canning handed down from a mother or grandmother. There may be business conventions that would include this skill and increase your target audience and customer base. You may be surprised, these skills passed down from earlier generations that you thought were a dying art, can instead become a nest egg of a market to tap into.

What skills do you have that could lead you into a successful entrepreneurship?

List the hobbies, knowledge and interest that you have that you could teach others how to do. Maybe it is playing tennis or the piano. Perhaps it is how to can food, crochet a blanket or sew clothes. I have encouraged three of my friends that enjoy photography into taking the path of a real estate photographer. Now they are busy and successfully photographing houses for the market for real estate agents, brokers and home owners.

They get to take a talent for something they enjoy and happily make money doing it. They had to get out there and solicit business, network and show off their skills and develop new ones. That, once again is part of the action step of Be-Do-Have.

Have

The happiest people don't have the best of everything, they make the best of everything

The final part of that is To Have. It is only after you discover who you are, your personality, your talents, the experiences that you had growing up that shaped and molded you, and the realization that you are still developing and have the ability to be who you want to be. That is when you have the opportunity to reflect on what you have; the joy in reaping what you have sewn. Appreciate what you have now, plan for the legacy you will leave for your children and grandchildren. If you want to have something else or something different or something more, then start the process over again. Figure out who you want to be or become. What are the action steps to get there and visualize what you will have, what it looks like, what hurdles you will need to anticipate facing along the way and remember to enjoy the journey? Enjoy what you have. This doesn't mean settling, or becoming stagnant in life. Continue looking for what you want even while being grateful and content for what you have.

Achieving Balance

In conclusion of this chapter, it is the Be-Do-Have attitude that you follow to rewrite your future. The Have is not likely enjoyed if you haven't enjoyed the experiences along the way. One way as discussed is to achieve balance on a daily basis. How do you find balance? Be here now..,.first and foremost. Take time to breath, relax and enjoy. Perhaps that is taking an hour out of your day to read a good book or soak in a bubble bath. I like to call that "taking in your oxygen". Take a yoga class, practice some Thai Chi moves in the new morning light, peruse a positive interactive website, and take a walk...

Whatever it is, you must take time out of your daily hustle and bustle to relax, decompress and refocus. If your daily energy and effort is focused on business, then your personal development, peace of mine and relationships will suffer. You must feed your mind, body, spirit regularly. You will find more joy and happiness if you are reaching and growing mentally, spiritually and emotionally. Also, that you spend time on you, individually each day for your own oxygen, then your family and friends, your business and your own spirituality.

Just like setting goals for achievement in business, you must write down examples or activities to fit each of those categories and budget your time for each. Just like a well regulated blood sugar keeps you feeling healthy and energetic, feeding vital organs to help them work efficiently, you must budget time, activities and attention to you and your relationships to achieve balance.

Right now, in your journal pages at the end of this chapter, take a few minutes to list a couple of activities and hobbies that help you to fill your own cup with a sense of accomplishment and satisfaction. What makes you feel good? This feeds your emotions. You cannot be successful nor interact well with others if you are neglecting yourself.

Rewriting your future is about your new and old relationships. Review what relationships are important to you? List children, family and friends. Make an effort to communicate with them on a daily or weekly basis. Connecting via text or email or phone call is good, but quality time spent talking face to face is even better. Schedule time with them.

Make appointments or the week will pass by and rain checks are made.

Lastly is your spiritual self. Set aside time to worship, to meditate and to whisper prayers of gratitude from your heart. More and more, people are ignoring and stunting their spiritual selves. It is just as important as our physical bodies and affects your daily fortitude to intentionally move forward in a positive manner. It is a part of who you are. It is where you draw your humility and your center for grace to forgive your past, heal and rewrite your future. We are human and make mistakes. We can learn from them and do things differently the next time, but our emotions are attached to the events, and sometimes we need to forgive others and ourselves before we can move forward and make a change. That comes from the mind, body and spirit. In order to decide and follow through with our future we need to understand that we are mental, emotional and spiritual beings that are connected to the actions and consequences from every experience from the beginning, middle and our future story.

In the song, "Becoming," by April McLean, it connects the process of healing. Yes, there were bridges that were burnt, feelings that were hurt. Since then, you were not at your best when it came to giving to another relationship. You had healing to do. You are becoming strong, healed and overcoming the past and ready to give to yourself, loved ones around you and perhaps another relationship. I encourage you to listen to the song and on the pages that follow this chapter, write the words, thoughts and feelings that stood out to you. Then as you identify within yourself that you are healing and overcoming, list ways you know this is happening within yourself. How do you feel stronger? What are ways you know that you are overcoming the negative and replacing them with positive attributes?

Activity

The next activity is to make a list of three people that helped you through your journey. These people stood by you and lifted you when you weren't sure if you could stand on your own. Perhaps they are a family member, a best friend or neighbor.

1.

2.

3.

Begin by using the pages at the end of this chapter to list ways they gave to you, performed a service great or small, and things you are grateful for. Take the opportunity to redeem your friendship and relationship by writing them a letter or email today. You are strong and would have survived, but this person helped you along the way and you may not be where you are today without their influence.

From Pandora's box sprung hope. Hope was born out of love and spawned the desire for something better. Exercise hope to be the person you want to attract in others, have hope for the best when making decisions and taking action steps to achieve goals, and have hope that what you have leaves an impression on the world, a difference maker, and hope you have lived a life and will continue to do so that will build a legacy for those you cherish. This is my prayer.

Date ____________

Date ____________

Date ______________

Acknowledgements

This book is dedicated to my children; no success can compensate for failure in the home. I have found success and failure in many facets of my life from business to relationships. The area I find of greatest joy in succeeding is being a mom.

Not just this book but my whole life, who I am and what I stand for I dedicate to my children. They are my rock, my pillar of strength, my joy and reason for being. We have supported each other through thick and thin and exchanged roles of teacher and student throughout the years. Following my dreams and setting an example is easy because of their love and belief in me.

About the Author

On the receiving end of an unexpected divorce while still in what she thought of as the "honeymoon stage", Janet felt like someone had died: her spouse and herself.

During transitional times in life, Janet understands first hand that it can be difficult to "shed the shadows", get back on your feet, go to work, and be involved. She helps the readers re-center, re-evaluate and refocus their lives to be more positive, productive and intentional each day.

She puts her education, 20 years coaching, and business owner, entrepreneurial skills to work to help the reader get to the other side of pain, where the future is dawning on a new and whole you. Janet has three amazing children and lives in Idaho. The Unwritten You is her second book; she is also one of the contributing authors of The Idaho Women Business Owners Success Stories.

Janet feels blessed and is grateful for all the opportunities to help people while building a business and hopes she can be an example of strong faith, strong hope and pushing through fear to success, in hopes to create a legacy for her children and grandchildren.